Exciting, Funny, Scary,
Short, Different, and Sad
Books Kids Like
about Animals, Science,
Sports, Families, Songs,
and Other Things

Exciting, Funny, Scary, Short, Different, and Sad Books Kids Like about Animals, Science, Sports, Families, Songs, and Other Things

Edited by
FRANCES LAVERNE CARROLL
and MARY MEACHAM

AMERICAN LIBRARY ASSOCIATION / *Chicago 1984*

Cover designed by Natalie Wargin

Composed by Compositors in Palatino
   on an Autologic APS-5 Phototypesetting system

Printed on 50-pound Glatfelter, a pH-neutral
   stock, and bound in 10-point Carolina cover
   stock by Thomson-Shore, Inc.

Library of Congress Cataloging in Publication Data

Carroll, Frances Laverne, 1925–
   Exciting, funny, scary, short, different, and
sad books kids like about animals, science, sports,
families, songs, and other things.

   Includes index.
   1. Children's literature—Bibliography.
   2. Bibliography—Best books—Children's literature.
   I. Meacham, Mary, 1946–   . II. Title.
   Z1037.C29   1984   [PN1009.A1]   016.80806'8   84-20469
   ISBN 0-8389-0423-8

TO *Rosemary Margaret Meacham-Zittel*

Contents

Preface

Exciting, Funny, Scary, Short, Different, and Sad Books Kids
Like about Animals, Science, Sports, Families, Songs, and Other
Things is an annotated bibliography of children's books that librarians suggest in answering children's requests for books. The title is
appropriate because this bibliography is arranged in divisions based
on the ways children generally request books: for example, "I want
a book about . . ."; "I have read . . . and want another like . . ."; and
"I like to read about . . . ." We found this to be a unique arrangement
when we were designing a format for the bibliography that could
express our idea to entice children to read the popular books recommended by librarians. Under more specific topics within these main
divisions are the lists of titles with short annotations that can be
used to answer children's normal requests. Exciting, Funny, Scary,
Short, Different, and Sad Books Kids Like about Animals,
Science, Sports, Families, Songs, and Other Things contains numerous and diverse lists of children's books for children to use, and
practicing children's librarians submitted the short, annotated, selected lists of fiction and nonfiction books. Not only the titles but also
the subjects are those that children prefer, as determined by children's librarians.

COMPILATION

The American Library Association (ALA) accepted the prospectus
for Exciting, Funny, Scary, Short, Different, and Sad Books

KIDS LIKE ABOUT ANIMALS, SCIENCE, SPORTS, FAMILIES, SONGS, AND OTHER THINGS in 1982; and in cooperation with Mary Jane Anderson, formerly the executive director of the Association for Library Service to Children (ALSC) of ALA, and Mary Ann Wentroth, formerly the children's specialist of the Oklahoma Department of Libraries, we selected approximately 125 names from the ALSC membership list and contacted these people in order to ensure that a large number of librarians participated in compiling the annotated bibliography. Half of the librarians we contacted in the first invitational mailing indicated an interest in the project, and we sent them a follow-up letter eliciting topics in demand. They were instructed to choose rather narrow topics instead of broad ones; the topics chosen for inclusion in the book are those suggested by at least two and often as many as six contributors. This book is unique in that the scope is based on approximately 100 topics in which the librarians know children are interested and for which they recommend these titles spontaneously.

We then compared these topics to a comprehensive list of approximately one hundred topics generally representing the main divisions of the Dewey Decimal Classification scheme, noted areas not covered, and reassessed the coverage. Contributors, in a second-round enquiry, were asked to respond to this general list of topics and to indicate any others that they thought should be included. They were also asked to revise topics that had been suggested but were considered too broad in comparison with others or were phrased as professional subject headings rather than like a child's request. In order to determine for sure that some topics were, indeed, being omitted because children are not asking for them, we made a third-round enquiry of local librarians for additions or omissions, based on forty topics we considered likely candidates for inclusion. It seemed that some topics such as computers (new) and dinosaurs (old interest) bore out our anticipation of topics that children ask for today, but some preconceived ideas of what children would ask for also were not shown to be valid. Books on football, submarines, and dolls, for a few examples, which we though might be popular, did not come up at all; and there were not any significant number of topics added to the original list. When the third survey was completed, we considered that sufficient effort had been made for what we wanted to know—whether children really ask for books on these subjects and how they ask for them.

We then directed each librarian to compile annotated lists of books on approximately five of the topics he or she submitted or was assigned (when several volunteered for the same topic) with selection of the titles based on the professional knowledge of children and books that each one had. We stressed that the intent was to supply an annotated list of books that *they often currently recommend to children*. The list could be of any length from five to fifteen books, but we reserved the right to add or delete any books. In a majority of cases two contributors submitted lists on each topic.

We reviewed each list to ensure that in its totality it is a fair representation of the topic and will be comprehensible and appealing to children. We also reviewed each annotation to determine that the language is natural to the children for whom the book is intended and that it possibly presents some new terms that will motivate children to read. The contributors were asked to include fiction and nonfiction titles in a list if possible, and many of the lists remain so without any concern for a balance between the two. Other lists tend to be either all fiction or all nonfiction, and the topic is a fair indication of why this happened.

Some titles appear on more than one list and have different annotations, although, in compiling the book, we followed a rather strict policy of elimination in order to avoid a popularity contest for a few of the titles. The title and the annotation had to seem to be best for inclusion on a specific list and were eliminated when they were marginal to that list. The number of titles by the same author on a list was also monitored, and the titles were culled to be sure the author was included for the title best suited to that particular list. The remaining titles by that author were omitted, with the reasoning being that the bibliography will introduce children to authors; and they can then use it to get at other good books by the authors they especially like.

ARRANGEMENT
AND CONTENT

The arrangement of the lists of books is by subject and is indiscriminative, as there is not any real reason from a child's point of view to put Halloween books with Christmas books, for example, together in a division of holiday books. (They ask for Halloween or Christmas books specifically.) Rather, we grouped only when we felt children might make an association, as with animals. The arrangement does not attempt to imply that the lists that come first are the most popular topics. It is primarily by subject as determined by children's phraseology of subjects; an exception is a reading list that encourages newly independent readers to choose somewhat easier material and locate it easily: these books could just as easily have been placed with a number of specific subjects. Within the lists the arrangement is alphabetic by title for the purpose of attracting children who do not as yet know very many authors.

The annotations are short, original, and written in a popular style that emphasizes the aspects of the book that appeal to children. Emphasis is on books for children in the second to fifth grades, and picture books are almost totally omitted with the exception of a few that seem to be appropriate for the grade levels specified. The maximum upper range is the eighth grade, as the intent is to cover children's, but not young adult, books. In the majority of the lists there are not any books that would reach this maximum. However, in lists that include contemporary realistic fiction, there are a few titles that approach this grade limit. Specifically, the list entitled "I Want a Book like Judy Blume's" may be used as a judge of what we consider to be books that reach beyond the fifth grade or do not fall into the heart of children's literature.

PURPOSES

Exciting, Funny, Scary, Short, Different, and Sad Books Kids Like about Animals, Science, Sports, Families, Songs, and Other Things should be valuable for parents, teachers, librarians, and children. It does not attempt to provide an overwhelming number of titles nor a lengthy treatment of each title. As one consultant said, "It is shaping up into a practical tool for the librarian on the floor." It is also intended for elementary school children to use as a personal reading guide. It was not feasible to provide space for users to write in the titles and annotations that they want to add under a specific topic, but we suggest this idea to owners of this book.

The majority of the titles are listed in *Children's Books in Print 1981–1982*, and the bibliographic entry in most cases is the same as the one that appears there. In establishing a publisher and date of publication for each book, we made every attempt to supply a reliable source for obtaining a copy of the book, although the purpose of this publication is not to provide a buying guide for librarians. The bibliographic information nearly always refers to the hardback edition although many of these titles are also available in paperback editions. Very few titles are out of print, but it seemed obvious to us as we looked at the lists submitted by librarians that they were using working collections that contain some out of print books children still read and love. We, therefore, included some out of print titles because this is valuable information to transmit, since users of this volume will be in similar situations.

There is a growing trend to become more aware of children's choices of books, particularly evident in the recent addition to *Booklist*, for example, of the column, "Chosen by Children." This trend is also evident in the state awards to authors based on children's voting for a favorite author. In addition, the responses that librarians make to children's requests are often expressed in the promotional brochures prepared especially by the children's departments of public libraries for giving to parents, teachers, and children, often to help select good books for vacation time reading. This title follows this trend by attempting to provide in an appealing format a longer, convenient, and usable listing of titles that recognize children's interests.

After compiling a first draft, we asked four people to make critical comments which we used to evaluate the manuscript further. The four indicated any need, in their perception, to add, delete, or revise. We are very grateful for all the assistance given by the many librarians who submitted topics, prepared annotated lists, and helped revise the manuscript. We are particularly cognizant of the value of having a good editor and want to express our appreciation to Herbert Bloom of ALA for his help.

FRANCES LAVERNE CARROLL
MARY MEACHAM

Acknowledgments

We are especially pleased to acknowledge the assistance from four librarians who worked on the overall manuscript. We asked them to read the entire manuscript for comments on the topics chosen to be included, the accuracy of the annotation in catching the flavor of the book, and the cohesion achieved in the titles suggested for each list. These people are closely associated with children and books, and they were most cooperative and extremely helpful.

Mary R. Somerville
Manager of Children's Services
Louisville Free Public Library
Louisville, Kentucky

Dorothy Jeffers
Librarian
Madison Elementary School
Norman, Oklahoma

Sue G. Justen
Public/Special Librarian
Seattle, Washington

Donna Skvarla
Head of Children's Services
Pioneer Multi-County
   Library System
Norman, Oklahoma

In addition, we wish to thank the contributors whose names follow for their responses with topics and annotated lists:

Ethel Ambrose
Coordinator of Children's Services
Central Arkansas Library System
Little Rock, Arkansas

Barbara M. Barstow
Children's Librarian
Berea Branch
Cuyahoga County Public Library
Cleveland, Ohio

Jean Bennett
Ludlow School
Shaker Heights City School
   District
Shaker Heights, Ohio

Anne Boegen
Coordinator, Youth Services
Miami-Dade Public Library System
Miami, Florida

Clara Bohrer
Head, Children's Services
Farmington Community Library
Farmington Hills Branch
Farmington Hills, Michigan

Linda Boyles
Children's Librarian, and
   Staff of Santa Fe Regional
   Public Library
Gainesville, Florida

Kit Breckenridge
Head of Materials Selection
Office of Work with Children
The Free Library of Philadelphia
Philadelphia, Pennsylvania

Elizabeth C. Breting
Consultant for Children's Services
Coordinator, Community Services
Kansas City Public Library
Kansas City, Missouri

Sybil Connolly
Library Media Specialist
Windsor Hills Elementary School
Putnam City, Oklahoma

Lucy J. Cutler
Lower/Middle School Media
   Specialist
Forsyth Country Day School
Lewisville, North Carolina

Elizabeth A. Dickieson
Chief of Department
Detroit Public Library
Detroit, Michigan

Laurie Dudley
Special Services Librarian
City of Abilene
Abilene, Texas

Kathy East
Coordinator of Children's and
   Young Adult Services
The Public Library of Columbus
   and Franklin County
Columbus, Ohio

Carol N. Euller
Webster Central School
Webster, New York

Virginia Lee Gleason
Supervisor
Springfield-Greene County
   Library District
Springfield, Missouri

Roberta E. Greene
York County Library System
York, Pennsylvania

Helen P. Gregory
Toledo, Ohio

Elizabeth C. Hoke
Coordinator, Children's
   Services
Department of Public
   Libraries
Rockville, Maryland

Emily C. Holman
Children's Coordinator
Ocean County Library
Tom's River, New Jersey

Dorothy Lee
Children's Librarian
Wilmot Branch Library
Tucson, Arizona

Charlotte Leonard
Coordinator of Children's
   Services
Dayton and Montgomery
   County Public Library
Dayton, Ohio

Jill L. Locke
Children's Coordinator/Branch
   Head
Farmington Hills Branch
Farmington Community Library
Farmington Hills, Michigan

Judy Mahan
McKinley School
Norman, Oklahoma

Penny S. Markey
Children's Services Coordinator,
  and Staff of the Los Angeles
  County Public Library
Los Angeles, California

Ramona Marten
Eisenhower School
Norman, Oklahoma

Alma L. Mehn
Collection Development Librarian,
  Youth Services
Palatine Public Library District
Palatine, Illinois

Patricia M. Patrick
Children's Consultant
Upper Hudson Library Federation
Albany, New York

Marian B. Peck
Head of Children's Services
Montgomery County–Norristown
  Public Library
Norristown, Pennsylvania

Barbara Ann Porte
Children's Services Specialist
  and Member Children's Librarians
Nassau Library System
Uniondale, New York

Barbara Quarles
Children's Librarian
Phoenix Public Library
Phoenix, Arizona

Linda R. Silver
Public Services Director
Cuyahoga County Public Library
Cleveland, Ohio

Anitra T. Steele
Mid-Continent Public Library
Independence, Missouri

Ellen M. Stephanian
Director of Library Media
Shaker Heights City
  School District
Shaker Heights, Ohio

Gail Terwilliger
Children's Coordinator
Cumberland County
  Public Library
Fayetteville, North Carolina

Becky Thomas
Librarian, Mercu Elementary School
Shaker Heights City
  School District
Shaker Heights, Ohio

Thalia-Manon Tissot
Division Chief
Central Children's Room
Brooklyn Public Library
Brooklyn, New York

Evelyn M. Wagner
Coordinator of Services to
  Children and Young Teens
Akron–Summit County
  Public Library
Akron, Ohio

Deborah Weilerstein
Coordinator, Children's Services
Arlington County Department
  of Libraries
Arlington, Virginia

Florence H. Yee
State Children's Services
  Coordinator
Materials Evaluation and
  Programming
Office of Library Services
Honolulu, Hawaii

We would also like to acknowledge the following people whose correspondence and telephone calls were appreciated.

Joyce Batchelder
Katonah, New York

Beverly J. Braun
Peninsula Unified School District
Monterey, California

Joan E. Cole
Flushing, New York

Margo Daniels
Tysons Pimmit Library
Falls Church, Virginia

Barbara H. Fischer
Wichita Public Library
Wichita, Kansas

Jennifer Fulkerson
Norman, Oklahoma

Darrel Hildebrant
Bismarck, North Dakota

Brenda V. Johnson
District of Columbia
   Public Library
Martin Luther King
   Memorial Library
Washington, D.C.

Barbara S. Moody
Enoch Pratt Free Library
Baltimore, Maryland

James A. Norsworthy, Jr.
Louisville, Kentucky

Charlotte B. Prechtl
Norman, Oklahoma

Marylett R. Robertson
Knoxville, Tennessee

Ryna H. Rothberg
Coordinator of Children's Services
Newport Beach Public Library
Newport Beach, California

Frances V. Sedney
Harford County Library
Belair, Maryland

Ristiina Wigg
Mid-Hudson Library System
Poughkeepsie, New York

I Want a
Book about . . .

ISLANDS

The Borrowers Afloat, by Mary Norton. Harcourt, 1959.

Arrietty and some of her family become castaways rather than face famine when the humans lock up the house and leave; for although it is a law that borrowers never speak to humans, they are dependent on them.

Call It Courage, by Armstrong Sperry. Macmillan, 1940.

Because Mafatu, a Polynesian boy, is afraid of the sea, the other islanders think he brings them bad luck. Mafatu flees to an uninhabited island where he overcomes his fear.

The Cay, by Theodore Taylor. Doubleday, 1969.

A young white boy and an old black man are washed ashore on the cay following a shipwreck. As Phillip gets to know the old man, he learns a lot about himself.

The Iceberg Hermit, by Arthur Roth. Scholastic, 1974.

When an iceberg rams his whaling ship, Allan Gordon is the only survivor. His home becomes the island of ice in the Arctic, and his companion is a bear cub. Do you believe he lived there one winter, two winters, or seven years?

Island of the Blue Dolphins, by Scott O'Dell. Houghton, 1960.

Karana and her little brother are left behind when their people are taken from their island. They are sure that another ship will return for them soon, but as the story, based on fact, unfolds, Karana is left alone on the island for eighteen years.

Island of the Great Yellow Ox, by Walter Macken. Macmillan, 1966.

Conor and some friends take his father's boat without permission and run into a storm. They manage to land on a little island and are stranded. That is only the beginning of their problems and of the mystery.

Islands and Their Mysteries, by George Laycock. Scholastic, 1977.

"Islands are magic places, little worlds of their own surrounded by water." This is the story of many of those places and the wonders of nature they contain.

My Father's Dragon, by Ruth S. Gannett. Random, 1948.

Elmer Elevator has fabulous adventures on Wild Island where he meets tortoises, boars, and tigers; crosses the river on alligators' backs; and rescues a dragon.

Swallows and Amazons, by Arthur Ransome. Merrimack Book Service, 1981.

The four Walkers finally have permission to camp out on an island and to spend a great deal of time sailing up and down the river. How can a holiday be better? Add some mysterious enemies, and you know the answer in this book that has been popular since 1931.

The Swiss Family Robinson, by Johann D. Wyss. Grosset, 1949.

The details of life on an island and of how cleverly a shipwrecked family manages have established this as one of the first and best of the castaway and island stories.

The Witch's Daughter, by Nina Bawden. Lippincott, 1966.

On the Scottish island of Skua, Perdita is called a witch's daughter. She makes herself known to Janey, who is blind, by a soft, warbling sound like a bird.

MUMMIES

The Buildings of Ancient Egypt, by Helen Leacroft and Richard Leacroft. Addison-Wesley, 1963.

Clear illustrations of the construction techniques including many cutaway drawings provide a fine introduction to the pyramids, tombs, temples, and homes.

Discovering Tut-Ankh-Amen's Tomb, edited by Shirley Glubok.
   Macmillan, 1968.
   The archaeological process and the people involved, especially
Howard Carter and Lord Carnarvon, are emphasized in a look at the
events surrounding the discovery of this famous tomb.

Mummies Made in Egypt, by Aliki. Harper, 1979.
   The techniques and reasons for the use of mummification in ancient Egypt are described with excellent drawings, many in color.

The Mummy of Ramose, by Shirley Glubok and Alfred Tamarin.
   Harper, 1978.
   Through the story of Ramose, much information about Egypt during the Eighteenth Dynasty and the life and death of a nobleman are
presented.

Pyramid, by David Macaulay. Houghton, 1975.
   Through detailed black-and-white drawings and an informational
text, the step-by-step process of building an Egyptian pyramid is
given. Preparation of the mummy for the tomb is also discussed and
illustrated.

Tutankhamen's Treasures, by John Ford. Chartwell, 1978.
   Among the many treasures found in the tomb of King Tut are a
solid gold death mask and carved pieces of an ancient game.

Tutankhamun and the Mysteries of Ancient Egypt, by Ron Knapp.
   Messner, 1979.
   The legend of "King Tut's Curse" as well as more usual informa-
tion about the tomb is discussed.

Wrapped for Eternity, by Mildred M. Pace. McGraw-Hill, 1974.
   The illustrations include actual photographs of Egyptian mummies as well as very detailed drawings showing the mummification
process.

SNAKES

A Boy and a Boa, by Abby Israel. Dial, 1981.
   When Martin's pet boa seems ill, he takes it to a friendly reptile
expert at a library program. The snake gets loose in the library.

Creepy Crawly Things. National Geographic Society, 1974.
With brightly colored, dramatic photographs and simple text the exciting world of reptiles and amphibians is introduced.

Discovering What Garter Snakes Do, by Seymour Simon. McGraw-Hill, 1975.
This tells how to handle a pet garter snake—feed and house it, take care of it, and how to watch its behavior to learn more about how snakes move, see and hear, and reproduce.

A First Look at Snakes, Lizards, and Other Reptiles, by Millicent Selsam and Joyce Hunt. Walker, 1975.
You can learn how to spot a snake, tell it from a lizard, know a crocodile when you see one, even tell one turtle from another.

Let's Look at Reptiles, by Harriet E. Huntington. Doubleday, 1973.
Lizards, crocodiles, alligators, turtles, and snakes are all reptiles. There are diagrams of their insides plus information and photographs about some of the more interesting ones in this book.

Meet the Giant Snakes, by Seymour Simon. Walker, 1979.
The lives of five kinds of pythons and the boa constrictor, what and how they eat, and whether they are a threat to people are described.

Poisonous Snakes, by Seymour Simon. Scholastic, 1981.
Only about 250 of the 2500 kinds of snakes are poisonous; among these are cobras, rattlesnakes, and vipers.

The Snake in the Carpool, by Miriam Schlein. Abelard-Schuman, 1963.
Betsy's lost snake is accidentally given to a neighbor boy with his birthday pajamas. They settle the ownership and learn together about caring for a pet snake.

A Snake-Lover's Diary, by Barbara Brenner. Addison-Wesley, 1970.
A boy who is so fond of snakes he keeps six as pets learns a great deal about them including the fact that it takes a great many rats, mice, worms, and dead birds to keep them fed.

Snakes, by Ruth B. Gross. Scholastic, 1975.
This is one of the best books for identifying common North American snakes. The first part of the book gives general background information on snakes.

Snakes, by Nina Leen. Holt, 1978.

The photographer-author spent a long time watching and photographing snakes to get these action-filled pictures. The text briefly describes some general characteristics of snakes.

Snakes, by Herbert S. Zim. Morrow, 1949.

Basic facts are given about the snake's body and how it works, how snakes find and catch their food, and how the young are hatched or born. Different kinds of snakes are identified in the drawings but not described at length in the text.

A Snake's Body, by Joanna Cole. Morrow, 1981.

What does a snake look like inside? It has no feet, so how does it move? How does it eat? The answers will be valuable information for future herpetologists.

Snakes: The Facts and the Folklore, by Hilda Simon. Viking, 1973.

After a general background on snake development and anatomy, different varieties are described. The range maps will be helpful, and many excellent, detailed color drawings make this a browsing book.

The Watersnake, by Berniece Freschet. Scribner, 1979.

Old Pitt, the snake, eludes capture by three boys who want him for a science exhibit; but in the process the boys learn a good bit about snake life and habits.

Where Can I Find
a Book about
My Body?

Are You There God? It's Me, Margaret, by Judy Blume. Bradbury, 1970.

Interwoven into this account of Margaret's small problems of acceptance among school friends and her religious identity is a great deal of information about a girl's physical changes in early puberty.

The Beauty of Birth, by Colette Portal. Knopf, 1971.

This picture book gives information on conception and birth, especially on the growth and development of the baby before birth, with a brief accurate text and very attractive, detailed watercolor illustrations.

Confessions of an Only Child, by Norma Klein. Dell, 1975.

As nine-year-old Toe and her parents have frank discussions about her mother's pregnancies, the premature birth and death of a baby, and the successful delivery of a baby brother, Toe learns in a reassuring way.

Growing Up Feeling Good: A Child's Introduction to Sexuality, by Stephanie Waxman. Panjandrum/Aris Books, 1979.

The direct text and frank black-and-white photographs (of children and teenagers playing and bathing, young lovers caressing, women giving birth) emphasize the wholesomeness of sex and good feelings.

Growing Up: How We Become Alive, Are Born, and Grow, by Karl De Schweinitz. Macmillan, 1974.

This offers a traditional approach to information on conception, prenatal development, and birth in animals and humans, with black-and-white photographs.

Learning about Sex, by Jennifer J. Aho and John W. Petras. Holt, 1978.

The text and pen-and-ink sketches answer all possible questions about sexual development, masturbation, intercourse, birth, and contraception.

Love and Sex and Growing Up, by Corinne B. Johnson and Eric W. Johnson. Lippincott, 1977.

Preteens will gain an understanding of the physical and social aspects of sexual development, intercourse, and birth. Heredity is explained, and the importance of families is emphasized.

Period, by JoAnn Gardner-Loulan and Marcia Quackenbush. New Glide, 1979.

A chatty, reassuring book about menstruation explains what is happening in your body, how to use pads or tampons, and how to deal with the physical and emotional discomforts that may accompany a menstrual period.

Where Did I Come From? The Facts of Life without Any Nonsense, by Peter Mayle. Stuart, 1973.

Frank, detailed information about male and female organs, intercourse, pregnancy, and birth with cartoon illustrations may startle some adults but help ease kids' tensions and embarrassment.

The Wonderful Story of How You Were Born, by Sidonie M. Gruenberg. Doubleday, 1970.

A lyrical text and soft pencil-and-wash drawings describe fertilization of an ovum, prenatal development and birth, and the growth of a baby.

Do You Have
Any Books
about Christmas?

Amahl and the Night Visitors, by Gian-Carlo Menotti. McGraw-
Hill, 1962.
  If you have never been fortunate enough to see and hear this short
opera, watch for it to be presented in your town or on television.
Meanwhile, read the story of a crippled boy, his mysterious visitors,
and the miracle that happened.

Baboushka and the Three Kings, by Ruth Robbins. Parnassus, 1960.
  The grandmother who would not go with the three kings to see
the Babe may seem very strange to us, but she is the central character
of a traditional story in Russia and other countries.

The Best Christmas Pageant Ever, by Barbara Robinson. Harper,
1972.
  The six fatherless Herdman children are the terrors of the town
and best avoided at all costs. So what were they doing in the Christmas pageant? Chaos reigns throughout rehearsals, and no one can
guess the final result.

A Certain Small Shepherd, by Rebecca Caudill. Holt, 1965.
  Jamie, unable to speak since birth, is extremely disappointed when
the Christmas pageant in which he is to play a shepherd is canceled.
When a husband and wife seek shelter from the storm, Jamie and his
family experience a miracle reminiscent of the very first Christmas.

The Clown of God, by Tomie de Paola. Harcourt, 1978.
  Giovanni is a famed juggler who travels throughout Italy to make
people laugh and applaud. When he is too old to juggle, he returns

to his birthplace in Sorrento. After watching the procession of gifts at Christmas time, he gives his final, inspired performance in the church.

Din Dan Don, It's Christmas, written and illustrated by Janina Domanska. Greenwillow, 1975.

The animals and birds with their musical instruments make their way to the stable in Bethlehem to greet the infant Jesus. The text is a Polish Christmas carol, beautifully illustrated by an artist who is Polish-born and has known the words all her life.

Father Christmas, by Raymond Briggs. Coward, 1973.

The author-artist takes you behind the scenes to watch Father Christmas (the British Santa Claus) as he gets up grumbling on December 24th, makes his deliveries, and returns home.

The Fir Tree, by Hans Christian Andersen. Harper, 1970.

A tree's brief glory as a Christmas tree in a fine house proves that it is wiser to savor each day of life rather than to wait for great things.

It's Time for Christmas, by Elizabeth H. Sechrist and Janette Woolsey. Macrae, 1959.

This collection of legends, customs, carols, poems, and stories is a rich presentation in which the authors emphasize the spirit of Christ's birth rather than Santa Claus.

Pedro, the Angel of Olvera Street, by Leo Politi. Scribner, 1946.

In celebrating Christmas with Pedro and his friends, you will probably sing with them, since both Spanish and English words as well as the music are given for the songs included in the book.

Do You Have
a Hanukkah Story?

The Hanukkah Book, by Marilyn Burns. Four Winds, 1981.

Hanukkah is the Jewish celebration in December in which candles are lighted for eight nights; and playing dreidel, eating special foods, and giving presents occur.

Hanukkah, Eight Nights, Eight Lights, by Malka Drucker. Holiday, 1980.

Forty-four candles are used during the eight nights, and many number puzzles for Hanukkah have the same answer: forty-four. Some of the puzzles and games are in this book as well as songs, crafts, and recipes to be used for this winter holiday which recalls a religious war that saved the Jewish people from extinction.

Potato Pancakes All Around, a Hanukkah Tale, by Marilyn Hirsh. Bonim Books, 1978.

Samuel the peddler vies with Grandma Yetta and Grandma Sophie with his recipe for potato pancakes for Hanukkah, the Festival of Lights. He wins, but their recipe is included in the back of the book.

I Like to
Read about
Kids like Me

AT SCHOOL

The Cat Ate My Gymsuit, by Paula Danziger. Delacorte, 1974.
School is so awful Marcy makes unbelievable excuses to get out of gym class; at home her father is harsh and lacks understanding. Suddenly everything changes with a new, swinging English teacher who predictably displeases the school board. Marcy, however, now has a cause and a new lease on life.

Chester, by Mary Shura. Dodd, 1980.
In Millard C. Fillmore school district everyone knows about Jamie's neighborhood because five of the kids live on the same street, are friends, and have special distinctions. When Chester's family moves in, the "records" are all shattered.

The 18th Emergency, by Betsy C. Byars. Viking, 1973.
With the help of his friend Ezzie, Benjie (known as Mouse) can cope with seventeen emergencies, but neither of them can figure out how to survive the eighteenth—meeting up with bully Marv Hammerman. Petrified by fear, Benjie finally faces the inevitable.

Freckle Juice, by Judy Blume. Scholastic, 1971.
Desperate to have freckles like his friend Nicky, Andrew buys a "recipe" for them from a classmate. The mixture produces a stomach-ache rather than freckles, so Andrew paints them on. His understanding teacher gives him freckle "remover" when his class reacts.

Getting Something on Maggie Marmelstein, by Marjorie W. Sharmat. Harper, 1971.

Several classmates are bothersome, but Thad Smith finds Maggie Marmelstein especially so. Maggie threatens to retaliate when Thad nicknames her "Mouse," and he and his friends must get something on Maggie "Mouse" Marmelstein.

The Hundred Dresses, by Eleanor Estes. Harcourt, 1944.

Wanda Petronski, a poor girl with only one dress, is teased because she insists she has a hundred dresses at home. Teasing can cause heartbreak, but just standing by and allowing the teasing to go on is almost as bad.

Jennifer, Hecate, Macbeth, William McKinley and Me, Elizabeth, by E.L. Konigsburg. Atheneum, 1967.

At her new school Elizabeth has difficulty making friends and is attracted to another shy classmate, Jennifer—a self-proclaimed witch.

Kitty in the Middle, by Judy Delton. Houghton, 1979.

Now in fourth grade at St. Anthony's, Kitty, Margaret Mary, and Eileen have been friends since first grade, and what escapades one doesn't think of another will. They crash a wedding in snowsuits and explore a haunted house.

Maudie and Me and the Dirty Book, by Betty Miles. Knopf, 1980.

Reading picture books to a first-grade class gets Kate and Maudie involved in a community censorship controversy.

Me and the Terrible Two, by Ellen Conford. Little, 1974.

Identical twins Haskell and Conrad move next door to Dorrie on the same day that her best friend moves to Australia. Not only are they neighbors but also they are all three in sixth grade. Dorrie survives numerous pranks and eventually discovers a basis for friendship.

Miss Nelson Is Missing! by Harry Allard and James Marshall. Houghton, 1977.

When Miss Nelson's class becomes the noisiest in school, Miss Swamp—in an ugly black dress—takes her place. She is a mean teacher, and the class yearns for Miss Nelson and promises to behave. Miss Nelson returns, but what about the black dress in her closet?

Nothing's Fair in Fifth Grade, by Barthe DeClements. Viking, 1981.

Jenifer is asked to show the new girl Elsie around school. This is not an honor as Elsie is gross. It takes the rest of the school year to work out Elsie's problem, but Jenny and her friends become more and more involved in helping.

Thirteen Ways to Sink a Sub, by Jamie Gilson. Lothrop, 1982.

Hobie Hanson's fourth-grade class thought it had a real advantage when the sub(stitute teacher) told them she had worked with kinder-gartners, but they soon learned that the sub was winning points in the battle between the boys and girls to make her cry.

The Toothpaste Millionaire, by Jean Merrill. Houghton, 1972.

Rufus befriends Kate as she adjusts to sixth grade in a new school. With Kate's help he makes and markets his own brand of toothpaste at an extraordinarily low price. Eventually the whole class and their math teacher back this engaging entrepreneur's venture.

What Do You Do When Your Mouth Won't Open? by Susan B. Pfeffer. Delacorte, 1981.

When her essay about America is chosen to represent her school in a county contest, Reesa is terrified. She will have to read her essay aloud to hundreds of people, and she has a phobia about speaking in public. Therefore, she must find a way to cure her fears in two weeks.

BEING BLIND

Connie's New Eyes, by Bernard Wolf. Lippincott, 1976.

A seeing-eye dog is shown in photographs from the time she is a puppy placed on a farm for obedience training to the time she helps her blind owner prepare for a new job as a camp counselor in Germany.

Follow My Leader, by James B. Garfield. Viking, 1957.

When Jimmie is eleven years old, an accident changes his life: one of his friends accidentally throws a lighted firecracker in his face. Blinded, Jimmie must learn Braille and use a guide dog to help him regain his independence.

From Anna, by Jean Little. Harper, 1972.

The other children tease Anna constantly because she never seems able to do anything right. Finally the doctor discovers why: Anna is nearly blind. She gains self-confidence after she receives glasses and special help in school.

Little Town on the Prairie, by Laura Ingalls Wilder. Harper, 1941.

Mary likes to be useful inside the house where she can see with her fingers, but she is also glad when she is able to go away to college. Her sisters are very sad when their blind sister leaves, and they decide to clean house for a week, just to be busy, while their parents are taking Mary to her school.

Secret of the Emerald Star, by Phyllis A. Whitney. Westminster, 1966.

The new Staten Island home of the Wards is in a small neighborhood where Robin soon becomes acquainted with Julian, son of a famous sculptor, and Stella, a blind girl. This acquaintance develops into a close friendship because Stella's cross aunt and a blackmailer give the girls a scary experience in which they can understand better Stella's physical handicap and Robin's desire to sculpt.

Sugar Bee, by Rita Micklish. Delacorte, 1972.

Stephanie (Sugar Bee) has potential as a poet, and her sixth grade teacher recommends her for a week in the Pennsylvania countryside with a family whose daughter Rosemary is blind.

The Witch's Daughter, by Nina Bawden. Lippincott, 1966.

When Tim and Janey go to the Scottish island of Skua with their parents, they do not expect to have dangerous experiences that relate to Tim's desire to be a detective or to Janey's blindness. Perdita, who is called the witch's daughter on the island, becomes their friend and this starts a treasure hunt.

BLACK CHILDREN

Cornrows, by Camille Yarbrough. Coward, 1979.

Close family ties exist when Great-Grammaw's and Mama's deft fingers weave their children's hair into the cornrow patterns of ancient Africa. They also tell folktales and talk about the accomplishments of the different clans until slavery fused them.

Daddy, by Jeannette Caines. Harper, 1977.

Wendy is so fond of her daddy that until he comes on Saturday she has wrinkles of excitement in her tummy.

Evan's Corner, by Elizabeth S. Hill. Holt, 1967.

Sometimes a kid in a family of eight just wants to have a place in this world to call his own. That's how Evan got his own corner. He made it his alone by adding a picture, a pet, and a flower; but he knew he could find peace and quiet there, too. However, Evan found he appreciated his corner most when he didn't spend *all* his time there.

The Hundred Penny Box, by Sharon B. Mathis. Viking, 1975.

Did you ever notice how you don't really mind if someone older, but someone you really love, calls you by the wrong name? Old Aunt Dew calls Michael "John," but he understands because she is 100 years old! She also has a wonderful old cracked box that has 100 pennies in it, and Michael takes care of that box for her.

The Jazz Man, by Mary H. Weik. Atheneum, 1966.

Zeke feels he has been abandoned when first his mother, then his father, and finally the jazz man and his music leave; and he goes to bed, lonely and cold. He is awakened by his parents who have returned.

J. T., by Jane Wagner. Dell, 1971.

In Harlem, J. T., a small boy, finds a new world of affection with Bones, a one-eyed, emaciated alley cat.

Jump Ship to Freedom, by James Collier and Christopher Collier. Delacorte, 1981.

Daniel Arabus and his mother, both slaves, should have been free because his father had fought in the Revolutionary War. Daniel escapes from their dishonest master and attempts to find help in buying their freedom.

Kimako's Story, by June Jordan. Houghton, 1981.

A boy with an arm fifteen feet long! This is only one thing seven-year-old Kimako describes when she dog-sits for one week and freely explores her New York City world.

The Lucky Stone, by Lucille Clifton. Delacorte, 1979.

These stories about slaving time and about emancipation are also about now.

Ludell, by Brenda Wilkinson. Harper, 1975.

A black girl's thoughts and experiences as she grows up in rural Georgia reveal her hopes and aspirations.

My Daddy Is a Cool Dude, by Karama Fufuka and Mahiri Fufuka. Dial, 1975.

Twenty-seven short poems depict life in an urban black community from a young girl's point of view.

My Friend Jacob, by Lucille Clifton. Dutton, 1980.

If you're small and have a big friend who helps you a lot, you feel good inside when you can help him. Sammy is only eight when he helps Jacob who is slower at learning, and he realizes the rewards of a "best" friendship.

Sam, by Ann H. Scott. McGraw-Hill, 1967.

The only way to keep little Sam out of mischief is to find the right job for him, one for which he is neither too little nor too big.

Sister, by Eloise Greenfield. Harper, 1974.

Thirteen-year-old Doretha keeps a diary of special memories. Sometimes when she adds to it, she reads back over what has happened to her. There are joys and sorrows and lots of reasons for her to remember "I'm me."

Song of the Trees, by Mildred Taylor. Dial, 1975.

Based on the author's childhood in Mississippi, the book tells of the struggle to retain black land rights when lumbermen try to force the family to sell beautiful old trees.

Spin a Soft Black Song, by Nikki Giovanni. Hill & Wang, 1971.

These poems are about children and what *they* think, feel, and do.

Stevie, by John Steptoe. Harper, 1969.

The universal experience of feeling rivalry occurs when Stevie comes to stay at Robert's house.

Striped Ice Cream, by Joan M. Lexau. Lippincott, 1968.

A poor fatherless black family with unconquerable spirit works together to make Becky's eighth birthday unforgettable.

Super-Vroomer, by Northern J. Calloway and Carol Hall. Doubleday, 1978.

If you and a bunch of your friends get together to build a winning race car, you'll be just like Jesse, Tommy, and Sarajane in this story! Don't forget the brakes!

Thalia Brown and the Blue Bug, by Michelle Dionetti. Addison-Wesley, 1979.

Drawing with a piece of blue chalk on the cement helps Thalia forget that her big brother never wants her to touch his stuff and that her baby brother gets all the attention. And that drawing leads to all kinds of excitement, just for Thalia.

Tough Tiffany, by Belinda Hurmence. Doubleday, 1980.

Tiffany, aged eleven, thinks she is tough. She worries about her mother meeting all the bills, about her sisters' bickering all the time, and about her half sister Dawn and the baby she is expecting. Granny teaches Tiffany about life way beyond booklearning—so in the end, Tiffany is "tough," loving, proud, and triumphant.

Train Ride, by John Steptoe. Harper, 1971.

Charles and his young New York City friends, curious about where the subway train goes, take an unauthorized ride to 42nd Street and back.

Who's in Charge of Lincoln? by Dale Fife. Coward, 1965.

Could you care for yourself (at the age of five) if your mother has to go to the hospital early to have a baby? Lincoln has no one to care for him, but he has his own adventure with a famous Lincoln in Washington, D.C. and returns home just in time find out he has a new brother!

Words by Heart, by Ouida Sebestyen. Little, 1979.

In winning the scripture-reading contest at the church, Lena hopes to make her papa proud; but it only adds to the resentment against her family, the first black family to move to Bethel Springs.

DOING FUN THINGS

A Bear Called Paddington, by Michael Bond. Houghton, 1960.

The Browns do not dream that one small well-intentioned bear (found on a railway platform with a placard around his neck saying, "Please look after this bear") can create such havoc in their household.

Fleet-Footed Florence, by Marilyn Sachs. Doubleday, 1981.

A girl who can run at superhuman speed is picked to play on a major league baseball team and becomes a comet in the heavens.

The Fourth Grade Celebrity, by Patricia R. Giff. Delacorte, 1979.

Feeling like a lump of vanilla pudding compared to her popular older sister, Casey Valentine expends all her energy becoming a celebrity in the fourth grade. She certainly does, but not quite the way she planned.

The Great Brain, by John D. Fitzgerald. Dial, 1967.

Imagine having the first flush toilet in your town. What a chance for a ten-year-old con artist to make some spending money selling admission tickets. Too bad his mother does not agree!

Henry Reed, Inc., by Keith Robertson. Viking, 1958.

Told in deadpan diary form, the story of Henry's enterprising summer in Grover's Corner, New Jersey, is very entertaining; he and his friend Midge strike oil, but it turns out to be a fuel tank that hasn't been used for twenty-five years.

Homer Price, by Robert McCloskey. Viking, 1943.

A doughnut machine that will not stop making doughnuts in a small Midwestern town soon creates an oversupply problem.

How to Eat Fried Worms, by Thomas Rockwell. Watts, 1973.

Billy really wants a minibike; and to get the money he needs for it, all he has to do is win a bet by eating fifteen worms in fifteen days. He can eat them any way he likes—boiled, stewed, fried or fricasseed—using mustard or ketchup if he wishes.

Mrs. Piggle-Wiggle, by Betty MacDonald. Harper, 1957.

Mrs. Piggle-Wiggle bakes sugar cookies for her friends who are all children. She also gives away puppies, loves to play dress-up, and thinks up good answers to problems that make sad people laugh.

Ordinary Jack, Being the First Part of the Bagthorpe Saga, by Helen Cresswell. Macmillan, 1977.

The other three children in Jack's family are always winning prizes and medals. Jack does not ever win anything, so his uncle thinks up a plan to attract some attention that nearly unhinges Jack's unflappable family.

Pippi Longstocking, by Astrid Lindgren. Viking, 1950.

Wild Pippi, with her stiff carrot-colored braids, lives at Villa Villekulla with her horse and money and is the strongest girl in the world.

Ramona, the Pest, by Beverly Cleary. Morrow, 1968.

Spirited Ramona starts school and loves her teacher but almost becomes a kindergarten dropout when she feels that Miss Binney does not like her anymore.

Soup, by Robert N. Peck. Knopf, 1974.

Rob and Soup are always in trouble, whether it is smoking cigarettes made of cornsilk or rolling down the hill in a barrel; but they are also good friends who do anything for each other.

Superfudge, by Judy Blume. Dutton, 1980.

Worm cookies, Fudge's disappearance, moving, and a new baby sister complicate Peter's life; but his funny, aggravating little brother Fudge has his good points, after all.

FRIENDS

Aldo Applesauce, by Johanna Hurwitz. Morrow, 1979.

Aldo gets a nickname when he spills the applesauce from his lunch at the new school he is attending. It is not easy to cope in fourth grade, but a special friendship with De De, a girl who dares to be different, helps.

Anything for a Friend, by Ellen Conford. Little, 1979.

Wallis (a weird name for a girl "they" always say) arrives at a new junior high school, only to be snubbed by the ruling clique of girls.

Bridge to Terabithia, by Katherine Paterson. Harper, 1977.

When Jess Aarons becomes a close friend of his new classmate Leslie Burke, they build a secret hideaway called Terabithia. Leslie's accidental death during a rainstorm leads Jess, in coping with the event, to new confidence in himself.

I Am an Orthodox Jew, by Laura Greene. Holt, 1979.

Aaron goes to Hebrew Day School, but his best friend goes to public school. Aaron cannot have a hamburger just anyplace with other kids, but he enjoys his family's observance of Jewish traditions including eating only food cooked under kosher conditions.

The Iceberg and Its Shadow, by Jan Greenberg. Farrar, 1980.

Anabeth experiences conflicts in her group of friends when the new girl Mindy ostracizes Anabeth's oldest friend Rachel.

Irving and Me, by Syd Hoff. Dell, 1972.

The move from Brooklyn to Florida is not to Artie's liking. Irving, his new, troublemaking friend, adds to his woes; but he becomes more accepting of the change after a series of experiences with a certain girl, bullies, and a very special dog.

Just between Us, by Susan B. Pfeffer. Delacorte, 1980.

Cass has a problem—she cannot keep a secret, no matter how hard she tries. Her mother, a behavioral psychology student, tries to help her; and Cass does well until she is caught in the middle by a secret involving her two best friends.

Let's Make a Deal, by Linda Glovach. Prentice-Hall, 1975.

Tony and Dewey are best friends and Lucy the dog is *their* pet until one family has to move to New Orleans. Where Lucy will stay is a big decision.

Me and the Terrible Two, by Ellen Conford. Little, 1974.

Dorrie is sure bad times are ahead when twin boys move in next door. But after working on a school project with one of them, she discovers she has made some new friends.

Philip Hall Likes Me. I Reckon Maybe, by Bette Green. Dial, 1974.

Is eleven-year-old Beth Lambert, who is always second best, letting Philip, her first love, be first? Of course, but she learns that she need not; and the two have lively adventures.

Rinehart Lifts, by R. R. Knudson. Farrar, 1980.

Nine-year-old Arthur Rinehart can't catch, can't throw, can't run, can't do anything athletic. His best friend Zan Hagen, who is athletic, wants to find just one sport Arthur can do and decides on weight lifting. Reinhart practices all through fall and winter for the grand finale, the Mr. Arlington Contest.

Tony and Me, by Alfred Slote. Lippincott, 1974.

Bill finds it hard to make friends when he knows his family will be in town only a year, but he finds it even harder to understand that his new friend Tony, who can help him play better baseball, leads him into a shoplifting escapade.

Truth and Consequences, by Miriam Young. Four Winds, 1975.

Kim vows never to tell another lie, and the stark truth nearly ruins her friendship with Alison.

Veronica Ganz, by Marilyn Sachs. Doubleday, 1968.

Veronica is a thirteen-year-old, oversized bully who terrorizes her classmates. When she tries to do the same to a new boy, undersized Peter, she not only has a pail of fish innards dumped on her head, but she also discovers something about herself.

Yours till Niagara Falls, Abby, by Jane O'Connor. Hastings, 1979.

Two friends vow to go to camp together until one breaks her leg. The other survives, humorously, and makes new friends on her own.

IN THE CITY

The Case of the Elevator Duck, by Polly B. Berends. Random, 1973.

An eleven-year-old likes to practice his detective work in his apartment house; but when he finds a duck in the elevator, he not only cannot find clues to its owner but also has to find a home for it.

City Sandwich, by Frank Asch. Greenwillow, 1978.

The interesting pictures and short poems are about many of the things and some of the people in a city.

Games in the Street, by Rachel Gallagher. Scholastic, 1976.

City kids like to play all kinds of games, and this book tells how to play them.

A Girl Called Al, by Constance C. Greene. Viking, 1969.

When you are fat and lonely, you may hide under a blanket of nonconformity; but your best friend (who lives in your apartment building) knows the truth.

Tales of a Fourth Grade Nothing, by Judy Blume. Dutton, 1972.

Peter's little brother Fudge (Farley Drexel Hatcher, age two-and-a-half) is his biggest problem. Fudge gets attention and his way by screaming. After he swallows Peter's pet turtle, he *seems* to understand that the new dog is for Peter.

Tar Beach, by Arthur Getz. Dial, 1979.

Lots of pictures help describe a summer Saturday in the city, including stairs, door-lock-release buzzers, and open fire hydrants.

Trouble on Treat Street, by Anne Alexander. Atheneum, 1974.

There is good reason not to trust strangers in a big city, and Clem and Manolo decide to be enemies at first sight. It was a nothing-to-do dumb day that they got together. Later when the two boys are brought home by the police, their families assume they are in trouble and should be separated.

Underground, by David Macaulay. Houghton, 1976.
Underneath a city are all the pipes, wires, props, and tunnels that make a city work, and this is an interesting look at how they all got there.

SUPER KIDS

The Boy Who Could Fly, by Robert Newman. Avon, 1976.
Going to live with their Uncle George and Aunt Janet could mean trouble for Mark and Joey because Joey is not an ordinary seven-year-old; he can read other people's minds as well as project his own thoughts to others who understand him.

Cam Jansen and the Mystery of the Stolen Diamonds, by David A. Adler. Viking, 1980.
Since Cam Jansen has a photographic memory, she and her friend Eric use her gift to help the police solve the mystery.

The Dog That Stole Football Plays, by Matt Christopher. Little, 1980.
During a football game Mike and his new dog Harry use their ability to read minds to learn the other team's plays. Is this fair?

Escape to Witch Mountain, by Alexander Key. Westminster, 1968.
Tony and Tia have powers beyond that of ordinary people. Tony can make strange things happen through his harmonica music while Tia, although mute, can communicate with Tony. Their search for their own people leads them into the high blue mountain.

The Headless Cupid, by Zilpha K. Snyder. Atheneum, 1971.
David's new stepsister Amanda volunteers to give him and his sisters and brother lessons in the supernatural. She conducts a seance in which the famous poltergeist of their house speaks. In another "happening" a dusty wooden head of a cupid rolls down the stairs.

The Hocus-Pocus Dilemma, by Pat Kibbe. Knopf, 1979.
Armed with a crystal ball, a fortune-telling book, and a book on ESP, B. J. goes into business for herself. When her predictions start coming true, B. J. is sure that she has ESP (extrasensory perception).

I Can Predict the Future, by Joseph Claro. Lothrop, 1972.

When eleven-year-old Max Turner predicts the outcome of a ball game accurately, he impresses both his family and friends; but when he predicts other things accurately, his friends become afraid. With the support of his family, Max learns to deal with his gift of clairvoyance.

Seven Spells to Sunday, by Andre Norton and Phyllis Miller. Atheneum, 1979.

Strange things begin to happen to Monnie and Bim after they write their names on the old mailbox with the seven stars on it: envelopes containing unusual things begin to appear in the mailbox for them, things which give Monnie and Bim extraordinary powers.

The Trouble with Jenny's Ear, by Oliver Butterworth. Little, 1960.

Jenny has an unusual problem: she can hear people thinking. This gets her into completely unforeseeable predicaments.

A Wrinkle in Time, by Madeleine L'Engle. Farrar, 1962.

Charles Wallace has an uncanny way of knowing Meg's thoughts; and when they and their older brother Calvin search for their father on the planet of Camazotz, Charles Wallace is the last to be rescued from the battle of minds because his is the most sensitive to the power of IT.

WHO CAN'T HEAR

Anna's Silent World, by Bernard Wolf. Lippincott, 1977.

Anna enjoys all the things that other six-year-olds do; but because she is deaf, she has to work hard to learn how to speak and to understand other people. She wears special aids that amplify sound so that she can hear some things.

Apple Is My Sign, by Mary Riskind. Houghton, 1981.

After his first term at a school for the deaf in Philadelphia in 1899, ten-year-old Harry returns to his deaf family's apple farm for a vacation. The spell-down and almost being hit by a train are stories he knows he will tell the boys at school when he leaves home again at the end of the summer.

A Button in Her Ear, by Ada B. Litchfield. Albert Whitman, 1976.

Angela's hearing problem is recognized when she throws the baseball to the wrong person and loses the game. Buzzie is so mad he says he will get her for this mistake, and she hears it as he will give her a kiss. After she gets a hearing aid, she finds she can tune Buzzie in or out.

Child of the Silent Night, by Edith F. Hunter. Houghton, 1963.

Almost fifty years before Helen Keller learned to communicate, Laura Bridgeman was known throughout the United States and Europe as the first deaf-blind child to be successfully educated.

Cindy: A Hearing Ear Dog, by Patricia Curtis. Dutton, 1981.

Just as a dog learns to help the blind, a small gray dog, rescued from an animal shelter, easily learns to alert a person to such everyday sounds as an alarm clock, doorbell, or smoke alarm. Her biggest challenge is accepting her new owner, a deaf teenage girl.

David in Silence, by Veronica Robinson. Harper, 1965.

To the children in his new neighborhood who have never known a deaf person, David is a curiosity until Michael makes friends with him and teaches the others to respect him.

Handtalk: An ABC of Finger Spelling and Sign Language, by Remy Charlip and others. Scholastic, 1974.

Expressive color photographs show people using their eyes, faces, hands, and bodies to communicate.

The Helen Keller Story, by Catherine O. Peare. Harper, 1959.

Deaf and blind, Helen Keller was unmanageable until the arrival of her teacher Anne Sullivan. It was she who helped Helen develop her abilities to their fullest. A remarkable woman, Helen Keller overcame her handicaps and worked continuously to help others.

The Mystery of the Boy Next Door, by Elizabeth R. Montgomery. Garrard, 1978.

The children in Joe's new neighborhood are angry because he ignores them and acts unfriendly. When the children discover he is deaf, they want to learn to talk to him.

The Swing, by Emily Hanlon. Bradbury, 1979.

Beth, eleven and deaf, and Danny, thirteen, live on neighboring farms, but they have never been friends. The only thing they have in common is a swing behind their houses. Then, after a close escape from an angry bear, they become friends, after being real enemies, because the swing means so much to them individually.

WITH HANDICAPS

Angie and Me, by Rebecca C. Jones. Macmillan, 1981.

Because twelve-year-old Jenna has juvenile rheumatoid arthritis, she must spend the summer in the hospital for treatment. With the help of the other children in the ward, Jenna learns about true courage as well as how to deal with her disease.

At the Mouth of the Luckiest River, by Arnold A. Griese. Crowell, 1973.

Tatlek, an Athabascan Indian boy, is born with a misshapen foot, but he learns from the Eskimos to use dogs to pull a sled and becomes a good hunter. When their greedy medicine man leads the men to fight the Eskimos with whom they have usually traded, Tatlek and his friend Sayo outwit him.

The Balancing Girl, by Berniece Rabe. Dutton, 1981.

Margaret, though confined to a wheelchair, contributes to the school fair by using her talent for balancing things.

Between Friends, by Sheila Garrigue. Bradbury, 1978.

Jill's friendship with Dede, who is retarded, turns out to be more valuable then she first realizes; for it is Dede who helps Jill through a difficult situation.

Burnish Me Bright, by Julia Cunningham. Pantheon, 1970.

Monsieur Hilaire, a famous mime, teaches Auguste, a mute orphan, his art before he dies; and Auguste shares his "magic" with two children. The rest of the people in the village punish him because they think he is using witchcraft and causing their misfortunes.

Don't Feel Sorry for Paul, by Bernard Wolf. Lippincott, 1974.

Although he was born with his hands and feet incompletely formed, Paul rides a bike, plays football, goes to school, loves baseball games, and wins prizes as a horseback rider.

The Door in the Wall, by Marguerite de Angeli. Doubleday, 1949.

Robin, the son of a nobleman of fourteenth-century England, is crippled by a mysterious disease; and his plans to be a page and eventually a knight are changed. He learns many skills at the hospice of St. Mark and understands what Brother Luke means when he says to remember that even crutches can be a door in a wall.

Feeling Free, by Mary B. Sullivan and others. Addison-Wesley, 1979.

Living with cerebral palsy, blindness, dwarfism, deafness, and other learning disabilities presents problems for the five children from the TV show "Feeling Free." Plays, stories, and things to do help you learn what it means to be handicapped.

Howie Helps Himself, by Joan Fassler. Albert Whitman, 1975.

Howie's legs are weak so he has to be in a wheelchair. The day he moves the wheelchair without help is a very happy day.

The Jazz Man, by Mary H. Weik. Atheneum, 1966.

When a musician whose piano playing everyone hears and likes moves into a nearby apartment, Zeke, a lonely handicapped boy, starts to come out of his shell.

Just like Always, by Elizabeth-Ann Sachs. Atheneum, 1981.

Janie and Courtney are two very different personalities. Janie loves activity whereas Courtney lives in a fantasy world; but by the time they come out of the hospital where they are both being treated for scoliosis, they are the best of friends.

Kelly's Creek, by Doris B. Smith. Harper, 1975.

Kelly has such a hard time making his eyes, hands, and brain all work together that other people think he is lazy. With the help of a friend who opens up the fascinating biological world of a creek, Kelly learns something important about himself.

Let the Balloon Go, by Ivan Southall. St. Martin's, 1968.

John's body is uncoordinated, but there is nothing wrong with his mind. One day when he is all alone, he decides that this is the day he will climb a tree. With strength of will and great effort he commands his body to climb.

Like It Is: Facts and Feelings about Handicaps from Kids Who Know, by Barbara Adams. Walker, 1979.

Children discuss their handicaps and how they have learned to live with them.

The Man from the Sky, by Avi. Knopf, 1980.

Troubled by a reading problem, Jamie struggles to decipher the word that will help rescue Gillian, who has been kidnapped by a man from the sky.

Mine for Keeps, by Jean Little. Little, 1962.

After five years at a school for handicapped children, Sally feels frightened and helpless when she returns to live with normal children. Her fears disappear with her family's help, a dog named Susie, and some new friends.

My Brother Steven Is Retarded, by Harriet L. Sobol. Macmillan, 1977.

Beth, who is eleven, shares her feelings about her brother Steven, who is not able to learn or understand things like everyone else.

My Friend Jacob, by Lucille Clifton. Dutton, 1980.

Though Jacob is older, bigger, and does not learn easily, he and Sam are good friends and learn from one another.

P.S. Write Soon, by Colby Rodowsky. Watts, 1978.

When Tanner writes to her pen pal Jessie Lee, she never mentions that she wears a leg brace and cannot do many of the things she writes about. It is her new sister-in-law Cheryl who helps Tanner confront her disability.

Ride the Red Cycle, by Harriette G. Robinet. Houghton, 1980.

After thinking about his decision a long time, Jerome decides he will ask for an adult tricycle (not a bicycle or a motorcycle which he would like) which will be sufficiently difficult for him to learn to ride with his leg braces even though he is eleven years old.

Sorrow's Song, by Larry Callen. Little, 1979.

Sorrow, who must write her messages since she cannot speak, and Pinch, a neighbor boy who is her friend, protect the white crane from the Zoo Man, John Barrow, an opportunist; and the hungry Sweets, all trying to capture it for different purposes.

Take Wing, by Jean Little. Little, 1968.

When Aunt Jessica comes to run the house while Mother is in the hospital, Laurel's family faces up to the fact that seven-year-old James is really mentally handicapped.

Welcome Home, Jellybean, by Marlene F. Shyer. Scribner, 1978.

After nearly thirteen years in institutions, Neil's mentally retarded sister Gerri comes home to live. Neil finds that living with Gerri, whose nickname is Jellybean, can be both frustrating and wonderful.

What If They Knew, by Patricia Hermes. Harcourt, 1980.

Jeremy is scared she will lose her new friends when school starts and they discover her secret (that she must take medicine for epilepsy). She has to think through what friendship really is when she is asked to give the "Address to the Parents" at her new school.

I Want a
Scary Book

GHOSTS

The Court of the Stone Children, by Eleanor Cameron. Dutton, 1973.

In an art museum Nina encounters the ghost of a girl who lived 100 years ago.

Echoes in an Empty Room, by Carolyn Lane. Holt, 1981.

Ghostly faces appear at windows, lonely deserted mansions unexpectedly show lights; there are also the sounds of dancing and mysterious disappearances.

The Ghost Belonged to Me, by Richard Peck. Viking, 1975.

With the aid of his friend/enemy Blossom Culp, thirteen-year-old Alexander Armsworth confronts the sobbing restless ghost in the family barn.

The Ghost of Thomas Kempe, by Penelope Lively. Dutton, 1973.

James Harrison is blamed for the pranks of the sorcerer, Thomas Kempe, whose spirit is loosened when an old bottle is broken in an English cottage. James must find an exorcist to clear his name.

The Ghost on Saturday Night, by Sid Fleischman. Little, 1974.

Opie gets involved in a "ghost raising" by a stranger who calls himself Professor Pepper. Opie and the sheriff outfox the professor when they discover his connections with a bank robbery.

Ghosts, by Seymour Simon. Lippincott, 1976.

Two of the nine stories, "The Ghostly Hitchhikers" and "The Restless Coffins," are examples of how things keep moving (sorry for the pun) in a supernatural world.

Scary Stories to Tell in the Dark, by Alvin Schwartz. Harper, 1981.

These stories of haunted houses, ghostly hitchhikers, phantom hearses, and grotesque bloody-fingered apparitions send chills down the spine.

The Thing at the Foot of the Bed, by Maria Leach. Philomel, 1959.

Do you believe in ghosts? After reading this book you might find yourself convinced! It includes short, humorous stories of imagined frights, spooky stories of bloody heads and long-toothed strangers, and charms to ward off ghosts.

Witches, Wit, and a Werewolf, edited by Jeanne B. Hardendorff. Harper, 1971.

Ghostly visitors, evil murderers, lost murder weapons, and awesome revenge are spiced with a touch of sly tongue-in-cheek humor for midnight reading.

SCARY STORIES AND POEMS

Devil's Donkey, by Bill Brittain. Harper, 1981.

Dan is the kind of boy who does not believe in magic or witches until one day he foolishly tampers with the "coven tree" and sinister old Magda, the last witch in the town of Coven Tree, puts a terrible spell on him.

The Goblins Giggle, by Molly G. Bang. Scribner, 1973.

Looking for something left in the graveyard, Mary is seized by a horrible walking corpse and forced to carry him away on her back! This gruesome story is only one of the frightening tales in this collection guaranteed to raise chill bumps.

The Haunted Night, by Joan Phipson. Harcourt, 1970.

Three girls face alone the increasingly alarming threats coming at them from the scariest haunted house around.

The Headless Horseman Rides Tonight, by Jack Prelutsky. Greenwillow, 1980.

These scary poems will trouble your sleep.

The House with a Clock in Its Walls, by John Bellairs. Dial, 1973.

The clock must be broken (it is programmed to destroy the world) and Lewis manages to outwit the scheme in experiences made more "shivery" by the house.

Inside My Feet: The Story of a Giant, by Richard Kennedy. Harper, 1979.

A *very* brave young chap sets a trap for the invisible thing that has come in very visible giant boots and has carried off his mother and father.

Nightmares, by Jack Prelutsky. Greenwillow, 1976.

These poems are the "stuff dreams are made of"—nightmares, that is. Vampires, mummies, zombies, trolls, and werewolves are brought vividly to life through eerie poems and sinister illustrations.

Squeals and Squiggles and Ghostly Giggles, by Ann McGovern. Scholastic, 1973.

Chilling stories with surprise endings, poems, tricks, and a diabolical skit are spooky fun for Halloween and all year long. "Feel the corpse," see into the future, and read about an eerie dinner party where nightmares become real.

The Tailypo, by Joanna Galdone. Houghton, 1977.

An old man alone in an isolated cabin, a sinister scratching sound at the door, and an eerie voice moaning for its lost tail combine to make this old Tennessee folktale a spooky story.

Whistle in the Graveyard: Folktales to Chill Your Bones, by Maria Leach. Viking, 1974.

A shivery collection of short, chilling tales about such horrifying creatures as "Jenny Greenteeth" and "Raw Head" is delightful for telling "under the covers."

The Wicked Pigeon Ladies in the Garden, by Mary Chase. Knopf, 1968.

An old abandoned house with a mysterious garden, a strange little man who disappears in the blink of an eye, and a group of sinister portraits that come to life lead nine-year-old Maureen into terrifying danger as she tries to escape the wrath of the evil pigeon ladies who are determined to regain their freedom-giving charm, a bracelet that Maureen has concealed in her shoe.

WITCHES

The Blue-Nosed Witch, by Margaret Embry. Holiday, 1956.

Blanche, a very young witch with a shiny blue nose, learns that it is great fun to go trick-or-treating with human children on Halloween night.

Dorrie and the Goblin, by Patricia Coombs. Lothrop, 1972.

Goblin is left in a basket at the door, and Dorrie finds that Goblin-sitting is hard work. Goblin goes into Big Witch's secret room in the tower and sits in her cauldron, spilling magic all over the house. Dorrie hurriedly "cooks a solution."

Jennifer, Hecate, Macbeth, William McKinley and Me, Elizabeth, by
   E. L. Konigsburg. Atheneum, 1967.

When Elizabeth moves to the suburbs, she has a new friend Jennifer, who believes she is a witch. Jennifer convinces Elizabeth that she can teach her to be one, too.

The Little Leftover Witch, by Florence Laughlin. Macmillan, 1960.

When Felina, a little witch, breaks her broom, she can't go home, so she is reluctantly adopted by a human family, but not before she causes a great deal of mischief.

Little Witch, by Anna E. Bennett. Harper, 1953.

Minx didn't want to be a witch's child, staying up all night, mixing brews, and never having to take a bath. She wanted to be like other children, go to school, and conjure up fairies, not evil spells.

Old Black Witch! by Wende Devlin and Harry Devlin. Scholastic,
   1980.

Nicky and his mother light the fireplace in the old house they have bought for a tearoom, and the black mess in the chimney turns out to be Black Witch, who thinks she owns the house. They give her a room in the attic, and she helps in the kitchen rather successfully. When two thieves (her kind of people) come, she realizes they are stealing from her, too; and she reverts and turns them into toads to make her room spookier.

The Story of Witches, by Thomas G. Aylesworth. McGraw-Hill,
   1979.

This history of witchcraft tells you that witches were believed to be servants of the devil, prone to causing mischief. They were real people, perhaps a little strange, but misunderstood and hunted unmercifully.

The Witch Family, by Eleanor Estes. Harcourt, 1960.

Amy and Clarissa, good friends, invent a family of witches: a wicked witch who likes to devour mermaids, a little witch who is very lonely, and a baby witch who has to be watched at all times.

Witch, Goblin and Ghost in the Haunted Woods, by Sue Alexander. Pantheon, 1981.

A goblin, a witch, a ghost, and a real ugly monster experience such problems as fear of water and nightmares and resolve them successfully.

The Witch's Egg, by Madeleine Edmondson. Houghton, 1974.

Agatha is a lonely old witch who lives in an empty eagle's nest where she watches horror shows on her only piece of furniture, a TV set. When an egg is abandoned in her nest, she decides to hatch it and acquires her first real friend, Witchbird.

Witch's Sister, by Phyllis R. Naylor. Atheneum, 1975.

Lynn is convinced that her older sister Judith is learning to be a witch and that she must protect her little brother because it is written in the books on witchcraft that witches are partial to the meat of young children.

I Like to Read about Families

ADOPTION

Aaron's Door, by Miska Miles. Little, 1977.

An eight-year-old adoptee, Aaron acts out his inner turmoil and fear of rejection by throwing tantrums, calling names, and barricading himself in his room. When persuasion fails, his new father forces Aaron to join them at dinner; and only then does Aaron begin to admit to himself that he is wanted.

Adoption, by Elaine Scott. Watts, 1980.

Reassuringly, the book answers questions about the adoption process, family conflicts, heredity, and biological parents.

The Boy Who Wanted a Family, by Shirley Gordon. Harper, 1980.

Seven-year-old Michael's year of adjustment prior to his adoption by a single woman, who also wants a family very much, is humorous; but there is also insecurity, doubts, and much reassurance.

Brothers Are All the Same, by Mary Milgram. Dutton, 1978.

Rodney, Nina's next-door-neighbor, does not think Joshie counts as a "real" brother because he was adopted as a toddler and looks different. Some typical kid-brother pranks convince Rodney that "brothers are all the same."

The Great Gilly Hopkins, by Katherine Paterson. Harper, 1978.

Can Mrs. Trotter, a fat and uneducated foster parent, win over eleven-year-old Gilly Hopkins? And what about the influence of the rest of the household: an odd younger boy and a blind black man? Will Gilly ever be able to say "I love you"?

How It Feels to Be Adopted, by Jill Krementz. Knopf, 1982.

A home to call your own is important, and adopted children have many different feelings as they fit into new families, sometimes still wondering about their biological parents.

I, Rebekah, Take You, the Lawrences, by Julia First. Watts, 1981.

Twelve-year-old Rebekah delights in having her own family at last, after years in foster homes and an orphanage, but finds some of the adjustment difficult and feels guilty at leaving her old friends at the home.

Is That Your Sister? by Catherine Bunin and Sherry Bunin. Pantheon, 1976.

Six-year-old Catherine, one of the adopted children, tells a true story about the problem of answering questions people always ask when a family adopts children of a different skin color after having their own.

Kate's Story, by Christopher Leach. Four Winds, 1968.

Kate is disturbed by her widowed mother's plans to remarry and by the discovery that she herself is adopted. Believing that a movie star whom she resembles must be her "real" mother, Kate sets out to effect a reunion but after many difficulties, realizes where her true family is.

A Look at Adoption, by Margaret S. Pursell. Lerner, 1978.

The reasons people decide to adopt children and why biological parents decide to relinquish them are given.

Me and My Little Brain, by John D. Fitzgerald. Dial, 1971.

J. D.'s desire to be a "Great Brain" is thwarted by the arrival of a hostile four-year-old, who is mute since he witnessed the accident that killed his parents. A well-deserved spanking finally loosens his tongue and eases tensions; and J. D.'s parents adopt the child, to everyone's satisfaction.

The Pinballs, by Betsy C. Byars. Harper, 1977.

Harvey, Carlie, and Thomas are the pinballs; they have not been able to live with one set of parents like other children. They meet at Mrs. Mason's foster home and begin, with determination and humor, to help each other.

Rasmus and the Vagabond, by Astrid Lindgren. Viking, 1960.

Oscar is a tramp, but he is nearly perfect in Rasmus's eyes because he is a moderate butterscotch candy eater and the only one Rasmus, a runaway orphan, has for a friend.

Seven Years from Home, by Rose Blue. Raintree, 1976.

Conflict between brothers leads to accusations. Mark thinks his adopted parents love their natural son Peter best; Peter thinks they show favoritism to Mark. Mark's desire to find his biological mother brings on some family outbursts and an eventual clearing of the air.

Somebody Else's Child, by Roberta Silman. Warne, 1976.

Ten-year-old Peter is crushed when he hears an admired adult say he "wouldn't want to bring up somebody else's child." Peter's adoptive mother is able to provide reassurances, but the love shown by his friend to his injured pet brings greater understanding.

Somebody Go and Bang a Drum, by Rebecca Caudill. Dutton, 1974.

A young couple adopts, one by one, seven unwanted children of mixed parentage, and they gradually merge into a big happy family.

BROTHERS AND SISTERS

D. J.'s Worst Enemy, by Robert Burch. Viking, 1965.

Three Madison children, D. J., his older sister Clara May, and Skinny Little Renfroe, grow up in Georgia during the Great Depression. D. J., full of mischief, finally decides it is time to become a responsible member of the household.

Dear Lola; or, How to Build Your Own Family, by Judie Angell.
Bradbury, 1980.

Arthur Beniker is the oldest of six orphaned children who form their own family and set up a home of their own. Arthur supports them by writing a newspaper advice column called "Dear Lola." Everything is fine until their new neighbors discover some of the Benikers' strange habits.

Everett Anderson's Nine Month Long, by Lucille Clifton. Holt, 1978.

Mama marries Mr. Perry, but Everett Anderson keeps his name; and they don't mind. When Mama and Mr. Perry expect a baby, Everett is reassured that there is plenty of love to go around for all four.

From the Mixed-up Files of Mrs. Basil E. Frankweiler, by E. L. Konigsburg. Atheneum, 1967.

Claudia decides to include her younger brother Jamie in her plans to run away from home because he has money. Hiding out in the Metropolitan Museum of Modern Art is quite an adventure for both of them.

Give Us a Big Smile, Rosy Cole, by Sheila Greenwald. Little, 1981.

Rosy's Uncle Ralph had written a book about each of her talented sisters when they turned ten. Now it is Rosy's turn—she and her violin—but Rosy does not play the violin with expertise, and this is where the trouble begins.

The Headless Cupid, by Zilpha K. Snyder. Atheneum, 1971.

Putting together two families with a new marriage makes life interesting and full of problems. Amanda, stepsister to David and the other three in his family, dabbles in the occult. One question to be answered is the meaning of the headless cupid on the stairway.

Homecoming, by Cynthia Voigt. Atheneum, 1981.

Four children, abandoned by their mother in a shopping center, walk from Connecticut to Maryland to find a home with their grandmother.

I and Sproggy, by Constance C. Greene. Viking, 1978.

Sproggy, Adam's new stepsister, joins the family when Adam's father remarries. Both Sproggy and Adam are ten, but Sproggy is two months older, taller, and English. Adam has a difficult time getting used to her aggressive ways.

The Luck of Pokey Bloom, by Ellen Conford. Little, 1975.

Pokey's poor luck in winning contests is almost as bad as wondering why her big brother, whom she has always looked up to, is suddenly so grouchy.

She Come Bringing Me That Little Baby Girl, by Eloise Greenfield. Harper, 1974.

Kevin did not want a baby sister in the first place; he wanted a brother. Besides that, the baby is fussy, ugly with wrinkles, and gets entirely too much attention; but soon Kevin is showing her off to his friends.

The Stone-Faced Boy, by Paula Fox. Bradbury, 1968.

Gus is the middle child in a family of five. The others are all boisterous and outgoing, but Gus's emotions get driven inward. Looking for a stray dog for his sister Serena proves to be a good experience for Gus.

The Summer of the Swans, by Betsy C. Byars. Viking, 1970.

Charlie, Sara's retarded younger brother, becomes lost when he goes by himself to look at the swans on the lake. The intense search, in which Charlie is found, has a remarkable influence on Sara.

Talk about a Family, by Eloise Greenfield. Scholastic, 1980.

Genny is aware of the impending breakup of her parents' marriage, and she hopes the return of her older brother Larry from the service will bring the family together again.

The Trouble with Leslie, by Ellen Matthews. Westminster, 1979.

Eric knows his summer will be ruined babysitting with his three-year-old sister so that his mother can go to college out of town. Somehow Eric proves equal to the daily challenges, and his summer turns out pretty well after all.

Welcome Home, Jellybean, by Marlene F. Shyer. Scribner, 1978.

Gerri, nicknamed Jellybean, is coming home to live after spending all of her thirteen years in various homes for the mentally handicapped. What does this homecoming do to Neil, one year younger than Gerri, and also to their parents' marriage?

Wild Robin, retold and illustrated by Susan Jeffers. Dutton, 1976.

Robin runs away because he hates to do the chores and awakens in a fairyland where these things are of no concern. He finds there is nothing to do, and he especially misses his sister Janet, who is so upset that a fairy feels sorry for her and tells her the magic she must work to release her brother.

DIVORCE

A Book for Jodan, by Marcia Newfield. Atheneum, 1975.

After her parents decide to divorce, Jodan's mother takes her to California; and the nine-year-old misses her father. During a visit to him in Massachusetts he gives her a scrapbook of shared memories so she'll always have him near.

Daddy, by Jeannette Caines. Harper, 1977.

Windy enjoys a truly close relationship with her father, who comes to get her every Saturday. It's the most important constant in her world.

How Does It Feel When Your Parents Get Divorced? by Terry Berger. Messner, 1977.

The photographs convey the idea that the pains of divorce lessen as time passes. A young girl shares her feelings of guilt, anger, and frustration until she eventually understands her parents' divorce.

It's Not the End of the World, by Judy Blume. Bradbury, 1972.

Karen learns that divorce affects the whole family and that simply wishing something not to be will not change the facts.

Me and Mr. Stenner, by Evan Hunter. Harper, 1976.

O'Neill doesn't know where home is while she tries to adjust to her parents' separating and setting up new homes. She also has to adjust to her mother's new live-in boyfriend. Can you love someone new and still love your father too, she wonders.

A Month of Sundays, by Rose Blue. Watts, 1972.

Accepting his parents' divorce is difficult for Jeffrey; he and his mother move from the suburbs to New York City, and he sees his father only on Sundays. New friends, an understanding teacher, and different activities gradually help him to cope.

My Dad Lives in a Downtown Hotel, by Peggy Mann. Doubleday, 1973.

Though Joey hears his parents argue more and more often, he is not prepared for their separation or his dad's moving to a hotel. After much soul searching Joey realizes that he is not to blame and that his parents both love him very much.

My Other-Mother, My Other-Father, by Harriet L. Sobol. Macmillan, 1979.

Andrea's divorced parents have each remarried; and she and her brother now have a stepfather, a stepmother, and four sets of grandparents.

Robbie and the Leap Year Blues, by Norma Klein. Dial, 1981.

Not only does eleven-year-old Robbie have to cope with his parents' divorce, but he also has all the girls chasing him because it is leap year.

The Silver Coach, by C. S. Adler. Coward, 1979.

Chris and her little sister Jackie are sent to live with the grandmother they hardly know the summer of their parents' divorce. In the remote hills of Vermont, the girls come to know and love their grandmother and to adjust to the divorce.

A Smart Kid like You, by Stella Pevsner. Houghton, 1975.

Nina's first day in junior high is baffling enough; but when she discovers that her father's new wife is her math teacher, she is devastated.

The Trouble with Thirteen, by Betty Miles. Knopf, 1979.

When two best friends share everything, including a reluctance to become teenagers, their problem is compounded by the unexpected threat of their separation caused by the breakup of a marriage.

Veronica Ganz, by Marilyn Sachs. Doubleday, 1968.

Veronica Ganz may intimidate other classmates; but Peter, the shortest, holds his own and becomes her friend. Veronica also has problems at home with her mother and stepfather, and she and her sister are often disappointed when their real father fails to keep his promises.

FAMILIES

Amifika, by Lucille Clifton. Dutton, 1977.

Amifika's daddy is coming home from the army, and Mama is getting rid of things he will not remember or are no longer needed in order to make more room in their small apartment. Amifika does not remember Daddy, so how could Daddy remember him? Amifika knows the answer when he meets his father.

And You Give Me a Pain, Elaine, by Stella Pevsner. Houghton, 1978.

Andrea shows her resentment of the attention her older sister Elaine gets in the family through her temperamental scenes and self-centered attitude. At the age of thirteen, Andrea learns a lot about herself and being part of a family.

Arthur, for the Very First Time, by Patricia MacLachlan. Harper, 1980.

Uncle Wrisby and Aunt Elda open up whole new worlds for Arthur the summer he is ten, when he comes for a visit, leaving his mother and father free to prepare for a new baby.

The Cartoonist, by Betsy C. Byars. Viking, 1978.
Alfie has his own special place in the attic above the living room ceiling, where he can retreat from his family and work on his cartoons, but his hideaway is threatened when his older brother loses his job and moves home with his family.

Holding Together, by Penelope Jones. Bradbury, 1981.
February is usually Vickie's favorite month. This year, as well as her birthday and Valentine's Day, she has a part in the school play; but Vickie's mother is very ill and will soon die, and this brings the family closer together.

The Hundred Penny Box, by Sharon B. Mathis. Viking, 1975.
Michael's mother wants to throw out the old box because it is always in the way and "underfoot," but Michael knows his great great Aunt Dew will be sad if she loses her hundred penny box. It is not easy to hide it so that it will be safe, for sometimes Aunt Dew does not know him and sometimes she does not answer.

Just Like Sisters, by LouAnn Gaeddert. Dutton, 1981.
Carrie cannot wait for her cousin Kate to come and visit for the summer. She is often lonely and having Kate around sounds like fun; they can be just like sisters. But Kate is a disappointment, and Carrie doesn't like her, not at least until the end of the summer.

Kimako's Story, by June Jordan. Houghton, 1981.
Kimako likes to sit on her front steps with her family and watch the people on her street. She also likes to read, but best of all she likes to be outside with all her friends in the neighborhood. Once for a whole week, she takes care of a big, old dog that belongs to the woman down the block.

Look through My Window, by Jean Little. Harper, 1970.
Emily, an only child, is not enthusiastic about moving to a big house in order for her parents to care temporarily for a bevy of her cousins. Yet she discovers pleasure in the experience and meets a new friend, Kate, with whom she can discuss writing and Kate's life as a Jew.

Pieface and Daphne, by Lisa Perl. Houghton, 1980.

Pamela (Pieface) befriends a "bag lady" as her part of a class project to develop new interests. Trouble arises when her mother invites her cousin Daphne to visit, and self-oriented Pieface must learn to share.

Ramona Quimby, Age 8, by Beverly Cleary. Morrow, 1981.

The Quimby family is trying to make do on one-and-a-half paychecks so that Mr. Q. can go to college. Beezus is turning into a tempermental teen, Ramona and Willa Jean are taken care of after school by doting Grandmother Kemp, and Ramona has to put up with a number of things that seem unfair.

The Secret Life of Harold the Bird Watcher, by Hila Colman. Harper, 1978.

Harold's parents work all day, and at night his dad likes to watch TV. Harold feels he is a disappointment to them. He wants to be a hero—and he is in his imagination. Daring escapades are easy to envision at his favorite secluded spot on the lake shore. Then, his late night capture of a real thief makes him a hero. His father remarks, "We certainly are proud of you."

So Long, Grandpa, by Elfie Donnelly. Crown, 1981.

When Michael is upset, he knows that Grandpa will talk to him and help him with his troubles. Then Michael learns that Grandpa is very ill and will soon die. Everything is changed and yet nothing is, and Michael finds a way to say good-bye without anger.

Sometimes It Happens, by Elinor L. Horwitz. Harper, 1981.

Does your dad tell you to get a good education? Do you hear about the tough life he had growing up? Have you seen yourself rescuing children or saving the life of the Queen of France? Victor wants to do something daring—to be famous. He does become a hero, but the best part is learning his dad had also planned as a child to be a hero.

Unhurry Harry, by Eve Merriam. Scholastic, 1978.

If you're a dreamer, you'll understand Harry. His dad hurries him along so he won't be late for school, pushes him to get the dinner table set, and demands he get in bed quickly so there'll be time for a story. All the time many more exciting visions are appearing in Harry's head because he is not in a hurry!

GETTING OLD

Annie and the Old One, by Miska Miles. Little, 1971.
A Navaho girl struggles to postpone her grandmother's death, which is symbolized by finishing the rug that she is weaving.

A Figure of Speech, by Norma Mazer. Delacorte, 1973.
Jenny and her grandfather, who has lived with her family all Jenny's life, both go back to his family's farm in an effort to keep him out of a nursing home.

Grandma Didn't Wave Back, by Rose Blue. Watts, 1972.
Debbie knows that her grandma is changing so much that Debbie's friends do not want to come over anymore, but she does not want to face her grandma's move into a nursing home.

Grandmama's Joy, by Eloise Greenfield. Philomel, 1980.
Why is Rhondy's grandmother so terribly sad? Rhondy helps her grandmother to remember what is really important when a family must face serious change in its members' lives.

Growing Older, by George Ancona. Dutton, 1978.
Several old people relate their memories of earlier days with interesting photographs of how they look now and how they looked then.

How Does It Feel to Be Old? by Norman Farber. Dutton, 1979.
The pictures help to make you feel both happy and sad as a grandmother tells her granddaughter the good and bad things about being old.

The Hundred Penny Box, by Sharon B. Mathis. Viking, 1975.
Michael shares his room and his 100-year-old Aunt Dew's memories as she tells him stories from each year of her life as represented by pennies in her battered old wooden box.

The Lilith Summer, by Hadley Irwin. Feminist Pr., 1979.
Twelve-year-old Ellen and her seventy-seven-year-old neighbor take advantage of the fact that each was secretly hired to look after the other.

Maxie, by Mildred Kantrowitz. Scholastic, 1980.
An elderly woman feels lonely and useless until she discovers how many people depend on her to start their day.

Mildred Murphy How Does Your Garden Grow? by Phyllis Green. Addison-Wesley, 1977.

Mildred, a lonely ten-year-old in a neighborhood of mostly elderly people, discovers that someone is secretly living in a garage apartment across the street—and the garage is about to be torn down.

Our Snowman Had Olive Eyes, by Charlotte Herman. Dutton, 1977.

Sheila does not mind sharing her room with her grandmother because her grandmother is fun, knows about a lot of things, and understands ten-year-olds.

Sunflowers for Tina, by Anne N. Baldwin. Scholastic, 1970.

When sunflowers brighten a little girl's life, she realizes that she can be a sunflower and brighten her elderly grandmother's dreary life.

The Ups and Downs of Jorie Jenkins, by Betty Bates. Holiday, 1978.

Jorie barely recognizes her father after his heart attack, for he has changed to a quieter, more solemn person. However, Jorie learns that he is still her loving father although he is no longer capable of doing some of the things that he could.

STEPPARENTS

Don't Hurt Laurie! by Willo D. Roberts. Atheneum, 1977.

Laurie's pain from physical abuse by her mother is made worse by what seems a trap to her—no one she can tell that can help her—until she tries her stepfather's mother.

Everett Anderson's 1-2-3, by Lucille Clifton. Holt, 1977.

Everett explores his thoughts about having a stepfather and finally accepts the idea.

Hiding Out, by Thomas Rockwell. Bradbury, 1974.

Upset by his mother's plan to remarry, Billy runs away to live in the woods. Discovering that this can be dangerous, he returns home to find his mother and new stepfather waiting patiently for him.

I Know You, Al, by Constance C. Greene. Viking, 1975.

Al bares her feelings about being too plump, disliking her mother's boyfriend, attending her father's second wedding, and not yet having her period.

In Our House Scott Is My Brother, by C. S. Adler. Macmillan, 1980.
When her widowed father remarries, thirteen-year-old Jodi finds some of the adjustments to her stepmother and stepbrother difficult.

A Smart Kid like You, by Stella Pevsner. Houghton, 1975.
Imagine twelve-year-old Nina's surprise on her first day of school when the math teacher is her new stepmother.

Telltale Summer of Tina C., by Lila Perl. Houghton, 1975.
Twelve-year-old Tina's parents are divorced and both are remarrying. After some time Tina realizes that her new parents are very nice.

The Unmaking of Rabbit, by Constance C. Greene. Viking, 1972.
Paul, also called Rabbit at school, thinks his weekend has built up to be the worst yet. Saturday morning he manages to evade participation in a robbery planned by the school bully and his gang by pretending to be very sick at his stomach. Sunday should be better—visiting his mother and her new husband. It is actually boring, and he takes an early train back to his grandmother's.

A Year in the Life of Rosie Bernard, by Barbara Brenner. Harper, 1971.
Ten-year-old Rosie has a difficult time making adjustments to living with members of her extended family and with her stepmother Lydia.

Where Are the
Monster Books?

MISCELLANEOUS MONSTERS

Dracula, Go Home, by Kin Platt. Watts, 1979.

While working at his aunt's hotel, Larry does some investigating of a guest who not only resembles Dracula but who also is usually around when something eerie happens.

Everything You Need to Know about Monsters and Still Be Able to Get to Sleep, by Daniel Cohen. Doubleday, 1981.

Information has been gathered about such legendary monsters as vampires, werewolves, zombies, mummies, and other monsters that supposedly live on land and in water.

Frankenstein Moved In on the Fourth Floor, by Elizabeth Levy. Harper, 1979.

Mr. Frank is the strange new tenant in Sam and Robert's building. He experiments with wire and electricity and has lots of secrets. Is one of his secrets his real name? Can he really be Frankenstein and a maker of monsters?

The Great Green Turkey Creek Monster, by James Flora. Atheneum, 1976.

The whole town of Turkey Creek is about to be taken over by a monster vine, the Great Green Holligan Vine, until a boy playing a trombone finds a way to control it.

Great Monsters of the Movies, by Edward Edelson. Doubleday, 1973.

Photographs from classic monster films, such as *Nosferatu*, make this title perennially popular; the text provides film history.

Meet the Vampire, by Georgess McHargue. Harper, 1979.
In a brisk, tongue-in-cheek manner, the author presents medical, scientific, and historical phenomena that have contributed to the vampire legend. Black-and-white illustrations set an appropriately eerie mood.

Monster Maker, by Nicholas Fisk. Macmillan, 1980.
Twelve-year-old Matt, having gotten a job helping to create special-effect monsters for the movies, has problems with a gang of boys and with his growing feeling that the monsters are becoming real.

The Monster Riddle Book, by Jane Sarnoff and Reynold Ruffins. Scribner, 1978.
Every monster is in this riddle collection!

Monsters You Never Heard Of, by Daniel Cohen. Dodd, 1980.
Here's your chance to meet some of the lesser-known monsters such as the Jersey Devil, the Dover Demon, and the Hairy Hands! These stories of giant birds, invisible killers, and a 115-foot snake are sure to frighten and amuse.

Nightmares: Poems to Trouble Your Sleep, by Jack Prelutsky. Greenwillow, 1976.
Reading about these vampires, werewolves, ghouls, ogres, and other monsters will surely make you shudder.

SOS Bobomobile; or, The Further Adventures of Melvin Spitznagle and Professor Mickimecki, by Jan Wahl. Delacorte, 1973.
The Bobomobile is a marvelous invention of Melvin Spitznagle (boy genius) and Professor Mickimecki. Their machine can descend deep into water so the two adventurers set off to find the Loch Ness Monster.

Scarlet Monster Lives Here, by Marjorie W. Sharmat. Harper, 1979.
New in the neighborhood, Scarlet Monster hopes people will visit her; but after all of her preparations, nobody comes. Is it because she weighs three hundred pounds and has crooked fangs?

Terrors of the Screen, by Frank Manchel. Prentice-Hall, 1970.
In this excellent survey of the horror film, the author explains the special effects used in the films and talks about the plot, the directors, and the actors involved. A fascinating group of photographs is included.

Thump Thump Thump! by Anne Rockwell. Dutton, 1981.

Digging in her garden, an old woman finds a hairy toe. She decides to keep it—until the Thing comes to her house to get it back. Suspense is built with just a few words. . . .

MONSTERS

Big Foot, by Ian Thorne. Crestwood, 1978.

Lots of black-and-white movie stills describe one of the famous movie monsters. The plots of the great monster films, the original movies and the remakes, are in a popular book series under the titles of the films (*Dracula, Frankenstein, Godzilla, King Kong, The Wolf Man*).

A Book of Monsters, by Ruth Manning-Sanders. Dutton, 1975.

Twelve folktales, favorites from around the world, are about ugly, bad, brutal, human-eating monsters as well as a few friendly and kindhearted ones.

Clyde Monster, by Robert L. Crowe. Dutton, 1976.

Clyde Monster hates to go to bed because he is afraid that a person will jump out at him while he's asleep. His parents are finally able to convince him that people and monsters have an agreement not to scare each other.

The Loch Ness Monster, by Ellen Rabinowich. Watts, 1979.

There is a large lake in Scotland called Loch Ness, and a monster called "Nessie" may live there. Some people say she does not exist, and some people say they have taken pictures of her. She presumably looks just like a plesiosaur (a prehistoric animal). What do you think?

A Monster Too Many, by Janet McNeill. Little, 1972.

Two little boys, who are babysitting in the park, are faced with the problem of helping a monster who is too large for the pond and who wants to get to the river where it can be free.

Monsters of North America, by Elwood D. Baumann. Watts, 1978.

Are there other monsters besides the legendary Big Foot roaming around the North American continent? Baumann has found six unidentified creatures that inhabit the United States and Canada and presents accounts of the encounters with them.

Movie Monsters, by Thomas G. Aylesworth. Harper, 1975.

Some of the great monsters that were seen on the movie screen—King Kong, Wolf Man, Frankenstein, Dracula, and the Thing—are recreated through stories about them and black-and-white stills as well as costume and makeup techniques.

My Friend the Monster, by Clyde R. Bulla. Harper, 1980.

Plain, ordinary Prince Hal finds he has the sign of the rose of the Witch of the Woods after he meets Humbert, a monster from Black Rock Mountain. Hal visits Humbert in the Land Between and vows he will, when he is king, try to lessen the differences between peoples and lands.

The Mystery of the Loch Ness Monster, by Jeanne Bendick. McGraw-Hill, 1976.

Many illustrations add greatly to this account of "Nessie," the supposed monster of Loch Ness, Scotland. There are legends about this monster, first mentioned in 565 A.D.; possibilities of its existence due to the unusual land formation of this area; and speculations about the creature's appearance.

Real Life Monsters, by Martha D. Allen. Prentice-Hall, 1978.

Some monsters, such as the Abominable Snowman and the Loch Ness Monster, are still speculative, but the gorilla, giant squid, and Komodo Dragon have been proven to be real rather than just creatures in tall tales.

Science Fiction's Greatest Monsters, by Daniel Cohen. Dodd, 1980.

The best-known monsters from the famous radio show "War of the Worlds," some "Star Trek" television episodes, and such films as *Star Wars* are included as well as background information and illustrations on how they were created.

Space Monsters: From Movies, TV and Books, by Seymour Simon. Lippincott, 1977.

Black-and-white photos of the space monsters from the "War of the Worlds," "This Island Earth," "Lost in Space," and "The Outer Limits" are among those included.

Where Are the Books on Weapons?

Bomber Planes That Made History, by David C. Cooke. Putnam, 1959.

Beginning with World War I, this history describes many types of bombers from all the nations manufacturing them, with the use, operation, and specifications for each. Some jets are included, and black-and-white photos illustrate each plane.

Fighting Gear of World War II: Equipment and Weapons of the American G.I., by C. B. Colby. Coward, 1961.

Half of each page is a picture and half is text describing how weapons, tanks, and vehicles were used to fight the enemy.

A History of Firearms, by Harold L. Peterson. Scribner, 1961.

Guns, cannons, and their ammunition are described and illustrated by pencil drawings. Most of these weapons are antiques from around the world.

Submarine Warfare: Men, Weapons, and Ships, by C. B. Colby. Coward, 1967.

With the use of many black-and-white photos, the author describes the men, offensive weapons, and actions of ships. The submarines *Polaris* and *Poseidon* are featured.

War and Weapons, by Brian Williams. Watts, 1979.

Colorful paintings describe man's warlike activities throughout the centuries, beginning with Rome and covering the present time. Weapons and uniforms are illustrated and defined.

I Saw It on TV.
Do You Have the Book?

The Black Stallion, by Walter Farley. Random, 1944.

Alec Ramsey is shipwrecked on an uninhabited island with the beautiful black stallion he has been admiring. By the time they are rescued, Alex has befriended the wild horse and can, with the help of a retired jockey, tame and race the Black Stallion in the Chicago Match Race.

Charlie and the Chocolate Factory, by Roald Dahl. Knopf, 1964.

Charlie Bucket is one of the five lucky children who wins a chance to tour Mr. Willy Wonka's famous chocolate factory. However, any child who disobeys Willy Wonka during this visit will meet with grave consequences. The grand prize is awarded to the child who completes the tour.

Chitty Chitty Bang Bang, the Magical Car, by Ian Fleming. Random, 1964.

The Pott family saves the remarkable automobile, the Paragon Panther, from the scrap heap; and it repays them by taking them on flights and sea voyages.

Freaky Friday, by Mary Rodgers. Harper, 1972.

Annabel Andrews wakes up one morning to find herself in her mother's body—she and her mother have switched places during the night. For one hilarious day Annabel is a housewife and mother while her mother is a teenager with growing pains.

From the Mixed-up Files of Mrs. Basil E. Frankweiler, by E. L. Konigsburg. Atheneum, 1967.

When Claudia and her brother Jamie run away from home, they go to New York City's Metropolitan Museum of Art to live. Before she goes home, Claudia insists on finding the creator of the most beautiful statue she has ever seen.

Mary Poppins, by P. L. Travers. Harcourt, 1962.

After Mary Poppins blows in on the east wind and comes to stay as the children's nannie, ordinary life for the Banks family, especially Jane and Michael, becomes extraordinary.

Mrs. Frisby and the Rats of NIMH, by Robert C. O'Brien. Atheneum, 1971.

When Mrs. Frisby goes to the rats underneath the rosebush for help, she discovers a society of highly intelligent rats who have escaped from NIMH where they had been taught reading and writing while held for experimentation.

The Rescuers, by Margery Sharp. Little, 1959.

The mice of the Prisoners Aid Society decide to rescue a Norwegian poet from the dark and terrifying Black Castle and devise a clever scheme to do it.

Sounder, by William H. Armstrong. Harper, 1969.

Sounder's master is arrested for stealing a ham and some sausage to feed his hungry family. The dog is seriously injured at the time, but he remains with the family while his master is in prison. The family learns to manage on its own, but the young boy loses both his father and dog in death.

The Story of Doctor Dolittle, by Hugh Lofting. Lippincott, 1948.

A people-doctor turned animal-doctor sets sail with his animals to get away from the cold and to cure some terribly sick monkeys in Africa.

I Need a Book about My Pet

HAMSTERS AND GERBILS

The Battle of Bubble and Squeak, by Philippa Pearce. Andre
Deutsch, 1979.
Bubble and Squeak are two gerbils, a gift to Sid, much loved by
him and his younger sisters but not by their mother! A battle that is
often very funny begins—between keeping them or getting rid of
them.

Discovering What Gerbils Do, by Seymour Simon. McGraw-Hill,
1971.
The wild gerbil was recently introduced in the United States as an
ideal pet. How to care for and enjoy gerbils is explained as well as
food preferences, grooming habits, behavior toward others, and the
use of their senses. The pet owner is encouraged to observe the
gerbil's behavior and to draw conclusions about gerbils' abilities and
natural characteristics.

A Gerbil for a Friend, by Donna L. Pape. Prentice-Hall, 1979.
When gerbils are born to the first grade's schoolroom pets, Mark's
name is third on the list to have one. He gets Lucy, learns to feed and
care for her, and has fun playing with her.

Gerbils, by Arnold Dobrin. Lothrop, 1970.
Although the emphasis is on observing the behavior of gerbils,
good suggestions for pet care are also given.

Gerbils, by Alvin Silverstein and Virginia Silverstein. Lippincott, 1976.

This tiny, clean, ideal pet came to the United States as a new laboratory animal for scientific studies. The book gives interesting information about the nature and care of gerbils, their breeding, and their usefulness in studying human diseases. It is illustrated with photographs, including some of infant gerbils, one to twenty-two days old.

Gerbils and Other Small Pets, by Dorothy E. Shuttlesworth. Dutton, 1970.

The origin of each animal (gerbils, hamsters, mice, guinea pigs, and other small mammals) and how each became popular as a pet are discussed. Photographs of pets with their owners reveal some of their habits and appealing personalities.

The Great Hamster Hunt, by Lenore Blegvad and Erik Blegvad. Harcourt, 1969.

Nicholas, pet-sitting for a vacationing friend, learns a great deal about hamsters—especially how clever they are at escaping their quarters and how to find them! Best of all, his parents decide he may have a pet of his own now.

Hamsters, by Alvin Silverstein and Virginia Silverstein. Lothrop, 1974.

The history, habits, food needs, breeding habits, and disposition of these small, furry animals are interestingly presented with dozens of appealing photographs, including several of baby hamsters and how they develop. Important directions are given on how to handle these little pets and what tricks they may learn.

Petey, by Tobi Tobias. Putnam, 1978.

Emily's reaction to the illness and death of her beloved pet gerbil is eased by understanding parents who provide prompt happy memories and arrange an appropriate burial ceremony.

The 17 Gerbils of Class 4-A, by William H. Hooks. Coward, 1976.

It's easy to get hooked on gerbils! So writes Chris in his science notebook. He is one of the caretakers of a pair, and it's a funny story of how the class manages when the pair becomes nine, then seventeen, and seven escape.

The Tales of Olga da Polga, by Michael Bond. Macmillan, 1971.

Olga, a guinea pig, finds a home with the Sawdust family and wins a prize in a show.

PETS

Care of Uncommon Pets, by William J. Weber. Holt, 1979.
The veterinarian-author gives sound, detailed directions for caring for rabbits, guinea pigs, hamsters, mice, rats, and gerbils as well as for salamanders, chickens, ducks, tortoises, snakes, lizards, and budgerigars.

Great Pets, by Sara Stein. Workman, 1976.
At the beginning of each chapter a brief synopsis for each pet is included—cost, housing, special requirements, diet, care, tamability, and life span. The book has photographs, diagrams, and a final large section on building all types of homes for pets.

How to Raise Mice, Rats, Hamsters, and Gerbils, by Sara B. Stein. Random, 1976.
"Pocket pets," what they like to eat, what kind of home is best for each, and why they may get sick are described with fine photos in color.

Keeping Amphibians and Reptiles as Pets, by George S. Fichter. Watts, 1979.
The six reptiles and amphibians discussed are frogs, toads, salamanders, snakes, lizards, and turtles. Information is given on catching the pets, building terrariums, selecting which make the best pets, and keeping them all healthy.

Mice and Rats, by Fiona Henrie. Watts, 1981.
Tips on how to choose a pet mouse or rat, how to handle it and give it a good home, and how to recognize sickness are given. How to breed rats and mice and enter them in shows are also explained.

Mice Are Rather Nice, poems selected by Vardine Moore. Atheneum, 1981.
These fifty poems about mice include many that are humorous and some that are sad. Mice have to work hard at keeping alive, and some of the writers pretend that mice enjoy parties and holidays.

Pets, by Frances N. Chrystie. Little, 1974.
Simple first aid is included along with information on the care of a large variety of pets including small pets, wild animals, and large farm animals.

Pets in a Jar, by Seymour Simon. Viking, 1975.

This book is concerned with the small pets that may never recognize their owners: worms, water bugs, hydras, brine shrimp, snails, and others. After discussing collecting and care, the author stresses eventual release of the pet into its natural environment.

Rabbits, by Herbert S. Zim. Morrow, 1948.

A description of rabbits in their natural habitats is followed by sensible suggestions on pet care.

Rabbits: All about Them, by Alvin Silverstein and Virginia Silverstein. Lothrop, 1973.

Many black-and-white photos and a few drawings illustrate this very complete coverage of rabbits, their life in the wild, different breeds, and especially the care of pet rabbits.

Shelf Pets, by Edward R. Ricciuti. Harper, 1971.

This book covers how to care for a wide range of small wild pets, the largest being tortoises and guinea pigs and the smallest, insects. Housing, food, and the peculiarities of each species are discussed briefly, assuming that pets will be kept varying time periods including a lifetime.

Superpuppy: How to Choose, Raise and Train the Best Possible Dog for You, by Jill Pinkwater and Daniel M. Pinkwater. Houghton, 1976.

Thinking of getting a puppy or training the one you have? This book tells you how to choose, train, care for, and understand a dog.

Your First Pet, by Carla Stevens. Macmillan, 1978.

Cartoon illustrations give directions for the handling, feeding, and housecleaning related to small animals, birds, goldfish, kittens, and puppies. The boy or girl who accepts responsibility for a pet such as a mouse, gerbil, guinea pig, or hamster needs to know these simple rules for keeping pets healthy, clean, and safe.

A Zoo in Your Room, by Roger Caras. Harcourt, 1975.

This book contains information on the care, housing, and responsibilities involved with keeping over thirty types of animals in a bedroom situation. It stresses preservation and respect for animals and suggests that keeping the animal's home most like its natural habitat is the ideal situation to create.

Where Are the Dinosaur Books?

A Dictionary of Dinosaurs, by Joseph Rosenbloom. Messner, 1980.

This useful book lists alphabetically the known dinosaurs, with brief information and a drawing of each. The facts include size, movement, habitat, food, the meaning of Latin names, the dinosaur types, and the period of the Mesozoic Era in which each lived.

Digging up Dinosaurs, by Aliki. Harper, 1981.

Pictures and conversations of visitors in a museum and scientists at work, often with lively humor, tell how the study of dinosaur bones shows much about life millions of years ago.

Dinosaur Days, by David C. Knight. McGraw-Hill, 1977.

About twenty dinosaurs are described and pictured as they probably looked in the Age of Reptiles. The author describes how scientists study fossils of dinosaurs (bones, teeth, eggs) to learn about their world.

Dinosaur Time, by Peggy Parish. Harper, 1974.

A few facts are given for each dinosaur such as its size, what it ate, or if it had teeth; there is a picture for each and an easy way to say the name.

Dinosaurs, illustrated by Laurent S. Sant. Wonder Books, 1972.

This is one of the clearest examples of the method used by scientists to reconstruct the skeleton of a dinosaur.

Dinosaurs, by Herbert S. Zim. Morrow, 1954.

Zim discusses the bird-hipped as opposed to the lizard-hipped dinosaurs and traces the development of the thecodonts from which the two great groups of dinosaurs developed.

Dinosaurs! A Drawing Book, by Michael Emberley. Little, 1980.

Starting with a line, a curve, or a triangle, and adding more, one at a time, anyone can make a dinosaur! The pronunciation and meanings of Latin names are given, and the endpapers show all ten animals together in their relative sizes.

Dinosaurs and Beasts of Yore, verses selected by William Cole. Philomel, 1979.

When poets put prehistoric animals into our world, or us into theirs, imagine Tyrannosaurus Rex at the dentist's, a pterodactyl driving a car, or a boy daring to pinch a dinosaur to hear it roar! It gives you the shivers or the giggles.

Dinosaurs and People: Fossils, Facts, and Fantasies, by Laurence Pringle. Harcourt, 1978.

The science of paleontology, the discovery and study of fossils of extinct animals, is less than 200 years old. In recent years it is challenging some ideas earlier accepted as fact.

Dinosaurs and Their World, by Laurence Pringle. Harcourt, 1968.

Fossils found, identified, and studied continue to tell us about a fascinating world of dinosaurs that existed long before humans.

Dinosaurs of North America, by Helen R. Sattler. Lothrop, 1981.

More than eighty different dinosaurs have been identified as having lived in North America. This book is organized by the periods of the Mesozoic Era, and the various dinosaurs living in each period are carefully described and pictured.

Draw 50 Dinosaurs and Other Prehistoric Animals, by Lee J. Ames. Doubleday, 1977.

Reading ability is not necessary because each lesson consists of six to eight diagrams in which simple shapes are combined to form the finished sketch. Dinosaur fans will enjoy drawing their favorite species.

The Enormous Egg, by Oliver Butterworth. Little, 1956.

Nate one day finds a very big egg apparently laid by one of the family's hens. It has a tough, leathery shell and finally, after several weeks, it hatches—into a Triceratops!

How Did We Find Out about Dinosaurs? by Isaac Asimov. Walker, 1973.

The mystery of the dinosaurs that has puzzled scientists for centuries (why did all the dinosaurs disappear at roughly the same time?) is accurately described in the history of how scientists came to know what they know about dinosaurs.

If the Dinosaurs Came Back, by Bernard Most. Harcourt, 1978.

What would happen if the dinosaurs returned to earth? The author says that they could push away rainclouds but that they would never mash up people like asparagus.

In the Days of the Dinosaurs, by Roy C. Andrews. Random, 1959.

Clear maps point out the sites of dinosaur remains in the United States and in many other parts of the world. From the discovery of the first fossilized footprints in 1802 by a Connecticut farmer to exploration in 1922 in Asia, this book traces the history of these fascinating creatures.

My Visit to the Dinosaurs, by Aliki. Harper, 1969.

A boy tells about the trip he made with his camera to a large museum in which he saw skeletons of huge dinosaurs put together by scientists and learned about them.

The Rise and Fall of the Dinosaurs, by Anthony Ravielli. Parents, 1963.

Ravielli shares his wonderment of the mystery of these giant creatures who dominated the earth for 150 million years.

The Shy Stegosaurus of Indian Springs, by Evelyn S. Lampman. Doubleday, 1962.

Huck (Huckleberry or Weewino in tribal Klickitat) spends his summers with his grandfather. He is protective of his grandfather and George the dinosaur, who cannot explain his presence after 60,000,000 years because his brain is no larger than a nut; but it is difficult for Huck when George hides in his grandfather's tepee during the picnic.

The Smallest Dinosaurs, by Seymour Simon. Crown, 1981.

These dinosaurs seem to be very like some of today's birds although they did not fly. The author gives facts on the size, habits, and speed of each.

Tyrannosaurus Rex, by Millicent Selsam. Harper, 1978.

Some huge bones found in Montana in 1902, when assembled, belonged to the largest known meat-eating dinosaur, Tyrannosaurus Rex. The book has many interesting photographs and drawings of discoveries such as this.

I Like to Read
about Famous People

American Women in Sports, by Phyllis Hollander. Grosset, 1972.

Famous women athletes throughout the nineteenth century are highlighted in the fields of riding, swimming, track, tennis, ice skating, overall athletics, golf, and bowling.

Cesar Chavez, by Ruth Franchere. Harper, 1973.

Strange that such a gentle man could stir up trouble! All that Chavez wanted was fair play for others and himself. Is that too much to ask?

Columbus, by Ingri d'Aulaire and Edgar Parin d'Aulaire. Doubleday, 1955.

In spite of everything, Columbus insisted on believing that the world was round and on sailing across the Atlantic several times to try to prove it.

Diana Ross, by Patricia M. Eldred. Creative Education, 1975.

A talented and popular singer, Diana Ross, former member of the Supremes, continues her success in music and films.

Fighting Shirley Chisholm, by James Haskins. Dial, 1975.

These glimpses into the life of a principled woman who became the first black congresswoman provide a role model for young women everywhere.

Free to Be Muhammad Ali, by Robert Lipsyte. Harper, 1978.

An individualist and a charismatic sports personality, Muhammad

Ali stands for the right to be as you are. This biography is as candid as its subject.

From Lew Alcindor to Kareem Abdul-Jabbar, by James Haskins. Lothrop, 1978.
A basketball giant reestablishes his identity by taking a Muslin name.

Jim Thorpe, by Thomas Fall. Harper, 1970.
Thorpe, a Native American, did not know about football until he went away to school. His athletic ability is now legendary.

The Life and Death of Martin Luther King, Jr., by James Haskins. Lothrop, 1977.
Coverage of the controversy surrounding King's death, including the conspiracy theory, caps this panoramic view of his life as a spokesman for the rights of people.

More Modern Women Superstars, by Bill Gutman. Dodd, 1979.
Six top women superstars—Nancy Lopez, Janet Guthrie, Tracy Austin, Diana Nyad, Joan Joyce, and Carol Balzejowski—are written about and photos are included.

What's the Big Idea, Ben Franklin? by Jean Fritz. Coward, 1976.
He was always busy, and he liked to try out new ideas. One of his big ideas was the invention of the lightning rod. One of his big jobs was to represent America in France since he was America's best arguer, and America needed France's help in the Revolutionary War.

I Want a Book
Where Kids Have
to Do Things

FOR THE FIRST TIME

The Accident, by Carol Carrick. Houghton, 1976.

Christopher and his dog Bodger are on a walk to the lake when Bodger is hit in the road by a truck and killed. Christopher's first grief and guilt over the death of a pet are eased with the help of an understanding father.

Amelia Quackenbush, by Sharlya Gold. Houghton, 1973.

Making friends during her first weeks in junior high school leads Amy (also known as Amelia, Melie, and Pet) into shoplifting and lying, with seemingly no way to stop even though she knows she is wrong.

Are You There God? It's Me, Margaret, by Judy Blume. Bradbury, 1970.

Margaret has lots of demands for God as she begins to mature physically but not quite as fast as she would like. Moving to New Jersey just before school starts is another complication. And what is she to do about choosing a religion?

Beat the Turtle Drum, by Constance C. Greene. Viking, 1976.

Joss and Kate are sisters and very good friends. Joss begins saving her money in May to rent a horse for a week for her birthday in June. She is sitting on a limb watching her horse when she is killed. Kate is both sorrowful and rebellious in July, but by August, even though it still hurts, she says in her poem that she cries more softly.

Bridge to Terabithia, by Katherine Paterson. Harper, 1977.

Jess and Leslie befriend one another in rural Virginia and claim a woodsy area as the kingdom of Terabithia, but their friendship is shattered by Leslie's untimely death.

Dorrie's Book, by Marilyn Sachs. Doubleday, 1975.

Dorrie is a happy, only child with ideal parents and a beautiful hilltop apartment. Then triplets arrive and things are not quite ever the same. Dorrie writes a book of her experiences of having her status as only child changed.

From the Mixed-up Files of Mrs. Basil E. Frankweiler, by E. L. Konigsburg. Atheneum, 1967.

Claudia runs away from home with her brother Jamie to the Metropolitan Museum of Art to get away from the injustices of home. She learns to cope with life as she knows it without thinking of running away again.

Ira Sleeps Over, by Bernard Waber. Houghton, 1972.

It will be the first time for Ira to be away from home and without his teddy bear. When the ghost stories begin and his friend needs his bear, Reggie runs home for his, too.

Leave Herbert Alone, by Alma M. Whitney. Addison-Wesley, 1972.

Jennifer must learn how to make friends with an animal, in this case a cat. After many disastrous meetings Jennifer finds that moving slowly and letting the animal come to her seem to be the best method.

Lost in the Museum, by Miriam Cohen. Greenwillow, 1979.

Jim and his class go to a museum, and despite the teacher's warning some of the children get lost in their haste to see a dinosaur. Jim is relieved to find the teacher, and for the rest of the field trip they stay together because they are so glad to be found!

Nana Upstairs and Nana Downstairs, by Tomie de Paola. Putnam, 1973.

A young boy lives with a grandmother and great-grandmother and enjoys their company and love. In learning about death when his great-grandmother dies, he is able to accept the eventual death of his grandmother when he is older.

Old Yeller, by Fred Gipson. Harper, 1956.

Travis learns to tolerate a thieving yellow dog that ends up saving all of the family at various times. He finds he loves Old Yeller; and when he must kill him, he recognizes that the pain of some responsibilities seem overwhelming.

Ramona the Brave, by Beverly Cleary. Morrow, 1975.
Ramona Quimby at the age of six finds that being different at school does not always bring its rewards and having one's own bedroom requires some getting used to at first.

The Summer of the Swans, by Betsy C. Byars. Viking, 1970.
Sara is in the ups and downs of maturity when Charlie, her mentally retarded brother, disappears. In searching for Charlie, Sara learns to be responsible for her actions.

A Taste of Blackberries, by Doris B. Smith. Harper, 1973.
The exuberant Jamie and his friends are working on a project to rid Mrs. Houser's grapevines of Japanese beetles when Jamie's prank with bees takes a fatal turn.

TO SURVIVE

Bones on Black Spruce Mountain, by David Budbill. Dial, 1978.
Two boys climb a dangerous mountain to discover the truth about the skeleton in the cave and to prove their survival skills.

Call It Courage, by Armstrong Sperry. Macmillan, 1940.
In spite of his great fear of the sea, Mafatu, a Polynesian boy, sets out in his canoe with only his dog and his pet albatross for company. Surviving the sea and his adventures on the sacred island earn him the name "Stout Heart."

The Cay, by Theodore Taylor. Doubleday, 1969.
Stranded on a small Caribbean island when his ship is torpedoed and blinded by a head injury, Phillip learns not only to survive but also to be self-sufficient under the wise guidance of an old West Indian seaman.

The Curse of the Moonraker, by Eth Clifford. Houghton, 1977.
Cat, a cabin boy, tells of the shipwreck of the square-rigger *Moonraker* and the survivors' struggle to stay alive.

Fire Storm, by Robb White. Doubleday, 1979.
A boy suspected of arson and a forest ranger are caught in the

midst of a devastating forest fire and must battle for their lives, using all their combined knowledge of woods and fires.

Island of the Blue Dolphins, by Scott O'Dell. Houghton, 1960.

Karana and Ramo, her brother, are left alone on the Island of the Blue Dolphins in the Pacific Ocean when their tribe is removed; and when her brother dies, Karana begins her quest to survive alone, one that lasts nearly twenty years.

Julie of the Wolves, by Jean C. George. Harper, 1972.

Miyax, an Eskimo girl of thirteen, is forced to learn the ways of Amaroq, the wolf pack leader, in order to have food in her escape and walk to the port from which she plans to sail to San Francisco. Her choice of whether to go or not, when she reaches the port, is influenced by her affection for Amaroq.

Mayday! Mayday! by Hilary Milton. Watts, 1979.

After their plane crashes in the mountains, Allison and Mark, plagued by their injuries as well as by a pack of wild dogs, manage to fight their way down the mountain to get help for the survivors.

My Journals and Sketchbooks [by] Robinson Crusoe, [by Anie Politzer]. Harcourt, 1974.

All the gadgets and ingenious arrangements for surviving on a desert island are presented in this "newly discovered" sketchbook and journal of Robinson Crusoe, the fictional hero from the classic novel by Daniel Defoe.

My Side of the Mountain, by Jean C. George. Dutton, 1959.

Sam Gribley leaves his home to conduct an experiment in survival in the Catskill Mountains, where he lives off the land for a year.

North of Danger, by Dale Fife. Dutton, 1978.

A boy skis 200 miles through glacier wilderness to warn his father of Nazi occupation of their town.

River Rats, Inc., by Jean C. George. Dutton, 1979.

Joe and Crowbar are shipwrecked while riding the Colorado River on a raft, but they survive with the help of a wild boy whom they find living in the canyon wilderness.

Scrub Fire, by Anne de Roo. Atheneum, 1980.

On a camping trip Michelle and her brothers are separated from the grown-ups by a scrub fire and become lost in the wilderness of the New Zealand bush country. Survival brings out all of the children's resourcefulness and their hidden talents as well.

Stranded, by Matt Christopher. Little, 1974.

Andy, a blind boy, and his guide dog Max are stranded on a small island when their sailboat is driven onto a reef in a sudden tropical storm and Andy's parents are washed overboard and disappear.

The Terrible Wave, by Marden Dahlstedt. Coward, 1972.

The Johnstown Flood of 1889 took less than an hour to destroy a whole city. Megan Maxwell sees the wave coming; the next thing she knows, she is floating on a mattress. She finds refuge on a raft with other survivors and gradually learns to share responsibilities.

Trapped on the Golden Flyer, by Susan Fleming. Westminster, 1978.

Paul's trip on the *Golden Flyer* holds more excitement than he had ever imagined when the train carrying him west through the Sierra Nevada mountains becomes frozen to the tracks during a blizzard.

Two for Survival, by Arthur Roth. Scribner, 1976.

When their plane crashes, two boys must fight for their lives when it is discovered that one of the passengers may be wanted for murder.

Two on an Island, by Bianca Bradbury. Houghton, 1965.

Jeff and his sister Trudy, marooned on a treeless island within sight of a busy city, discover new respect and trust for each other as they endure hunger, thirst, and sunburn while awaiting rescue.

I Need a Book
for Science Class

INSECTS AND SPIDERS

Bees, Wasps and Hornets, by Robert M. McClung. Morrow, 1971.

The likenesses and differences of most of the membrane-winged insects (parasitic wasps, solitary hunting wasps, social wasps, and bees) and how they live are explained. A chapter on the importance of bees is included.

The Bug Club Book, by Gladys Conklin. Holiday, 1966.

This handbook contains directions for collecting, raising, preserving, mounting, studying, and displaying insects.

The Butterfly Cycle, by Oxford Scientific Films. Putnam, 1977.

Four pages of text describe the life cycle of the Cabbage White butterfly. Large-scale, color-captioned photographs show: laying of eggs, development of the caterpillar, creation of the chrysalis, emergence of the adult butterfly, and mating.

Cockroaches: Here, There, and Everywhere, by Laurence Pringle. Harper, 1971.

The first part of the book tells about the habits and habitat of this hardy insect pest. The latter part of the book covers the cockroach's life cycle.

Dragonflies, by Oxford Scientific Films. Putnam, 1980.

Enlarged photographs show the anatomy, life cycle, and habitat of two varieties of dragonfly and one variety of damselfly.

Insects, by Illa Podendorf. Childrens Pr., 1981.

What are insects? Where do they live? How are they alike? Insects may live alone or in large families, be good builders or fast runners.

Ladybug, Ladybug, Fly Away Home, by Judy Hawes. Harper, 1967.

Most children are familiar with ladybugs and can discover through this title where these beetles live, what they eat, and how they fly and walk. Besides explaining age-old superstitions about this insect, the author explains how ladybugs help to control other insect pests.

A Look at Ants, by Ross E. Hutchins. Dodd, 1978.

Ants are one of the most common of insects, yet one of the most fascinating. The book describes the habits, life cycles, and roles of queen ants, workers, and soldiers.

Questions and Answers about Ants, by Millicent Selsam. Four Winds, 1967.

Brief, clear, and scientifically accurate, this inviting book answers basic questions about ant anatomy and behavior.

Spider Magic, by Dorothy H. Patent. Holiday, 1982.

A few of the over 30,000 kinds of spiders from around the world are shown in excellent blownup photographs so detailed you can see the tiny hairs on a spider's legs.

The Web in the Grass, by Berniece Freschet. Scribner, 1972.

Daily activities of the common spider, spinning a web to trap insects for food, hiding from enemies, and laying eggs, are presented in story form with colorful illustrations.

PLANTS

From One Seed, by Vera R. Webster. McKay, 1977.

Seeds come in all sizes from the tiny mustard seed to the big coconut, but they all provide the means to make another plant.

Grocery Store Botany, by Joan E. Rahn. Atheneum, 1974.

You can do these experiments using the vegetables found at the corner market.

How to Grow a Jelly Glass Farm, by Kathy Mandry. Pantheon, 1974.

Directions on sowing a sneaker with grass; tossing together a dandelion salad; or, if you have a "brown thumb," drying decorative weeds are contained in this book along with other green thumb projects and experiments.

Making a Native Plant Terrarium, by D. J. Herda. Messner, 1977.

Use the step-by-step procedure on how to make a terrarium with small plants you gather yourself. Wild plants commonly available are also pictured.

Plants Do Amazing Things, by Hedda Nussbaum. Random, 1977.

Some plants eat meat, others move or glow in the dark; this book explains why and how certain plants can do these amazing things.

Seasons of the Tallgrass Prairie, by Carol Lerner. Morrow, 1980.

Most of the over 100 native plants growing in the Midwestern prairie are forbs (wildflowers). These and the grasses that are often described as a green sea are perennials, and they are part of America's living history.

Trees, by Herbert S. Zim and Alexander C. Martin. Western, 1952.

Colored pictures of the tree's shape, enlargements of the bark and leaves, and small maps make this guidebook easy to use in identifying familiar American trees.

Watch Out, It's Poison Ivy, by Peter R. Limburg. Messner, 1973.

Where it grows, what it looks like, and what to do when you contact poison ivy are covered in this book as well as its poisonous relatives and harmless look-alikes.

Wild Green Things in the City, by Anne O. Dowden. Crowell, 1972.

Arranged by seasons and illustrated in color, this book identifies the common wild flowers and weeds found in most urban areas. Lists of wild plants found in Manhattan, Denver, and Los Angeles are appended.

SCIENCE EXPERIMENTS

Berenstain Bears' Science Fair, by Stan Berenstain and Jan Berenstain. Random, 1977.

Papa Bear believes Small Bear and Sister must know something about machines, matter, and energy before they prepare their projects for the Bears' Science Fair.

Catch a Sunbeam: A Book of Solar Study and Experiments, by Florence Adams. Harcourt, 1978.

You will delight in these experiments with the sun and understand more about this energy source.

Dr. Zed's Brilliant Book of Science Experiments, by Gordon Penrose. Barron, 1977.

Although the comic-book format of this book may be confusing at first, Dr. Zed's book is loaded with terrific experiments that lead into the world of observation and discovery.

Fascinating Experiments in Physics, by Francois Cherrier. Sterling, 1978.

A splendidly illustrated book brimming with superbly explained (although not always easy to perform) experiments that include such wonders as—making your own solar furnace, a Cartesian diver, or even your own projector!

How to Do a Science Project, by David Webster. Watts, 1974.

Webster takes you step-by-step into the methods of formulating and presenting beginning science fair projects and experiments.

Nuts and Bolts, a Matter of Fact Guide to Science Fair Projects, by Barry A. VanDeman and Ed McDonald. Science Man Pr., 1980.

Practical tips on all aspects (choosing, outlining, and researching) are included in this book which is especially good on procedures for presentation of a project. A list of suggested sources of information related to choosing a topic and a list of award-winning projects are included.

The Reasons for Seasons: The Great Cosmic Megagalactic Trip without Moving from Your Chair, by Linda Allison. Little, 1975.

Experiment, cook, make dolls, make paper, even decorate a Christmas tree while you explore the fascinating movements of the earth, sun, moon, and stars.

The Secret Life of Hardware, a Science Experiment Book, by Vicki Cobb. Lippincott, 1982.

Each of the five parts, on cleaners, paints, connectors, tools, and electricity, has a two-page introduction, followed by four to seven experiments that are explained with a list of materials and equipment needed and suggestions and observations for after the experiment. The materials and equipment are relatively easy to obtain.

STARS AND PLANETS

Find the Constellations, by H. A. Rey. Houghton, 1976.

Large-sized, this book helps you recognize stars and find constellations in the night sky. The illustrations give a view of the sky as if you were looking out at night through an observatory window. It includes a glossary and several self-tests to see how well you stargaze.

Journey to the Planets, by Patricia Lauber. Crown, 1982.

All the planets of the solar system, including earth, and their moons are described clearly and interestingly and in great detail, with many recent satellite photographs.

Look to the Night Sky: An Introduction to Star Watching, by Seymour Simon. Viking, 1977.

For beginners in stargazing this book gives instructions on how to look at the stars and understand what you see. Various ways for finding constellations are discussed. There is also a discussion of the differences between astronomy and astrology and what you can learn from each.

The Planets in Our Solar System, by Franklyn M. Branley. Harper, 1981.

Asteroids and comets are also covered in this solid, elementary introduction to the planets in the solar system. There are directions for building a scale model of the solar system, and the illustrations include actual photographs, diagrams, and charts.

Planets, Stars, and Galaxies, by Melvin Berger. Putnam, 1978.

A straightforward, beginning overview of astronomy looks at discoveries and theories about planets, stars, and galaxies. It includes a glossary and helpful charts of important facts about each planet such as its diameter, orbital speed, distance from the sun, length of day, and length of year.

Stars, by Herbert S. Zim and Robert H. Baker. Western, 1951.

A handbook for the study of stars, constellations, and the solar system gives useful facts and information in a clear, colorful format. It includes many useful charts such as classification of stars and comparison of planets as well as many illustrations.

The Sun, by Herbert S. Zim. Morrow, 1975.

A useful beginning study of the sun covers its size, temperature, composition, distance from the earth, and solar energy. Sunspots are explained as well as how they affect us, and simple experiments and illustrations are included.

What Makes the Sun Shine? by Isaac Asimov. Little, 1971.

The origins of the earth and planets are explained as are the composition of the sun and how it produces energy.

VOLCANOES

Disastrous Volcanoes, by Melvin Berger. Watts, 1981.

Specific volcanoes (including Vesuvius, Krakatoa, and Mount St. Helens) are described.

The Earth and Space, by David Lambert. Warwick, 1979.

The section on volcanoes includes much useful information, a cutaway view of a volcano, and a map of the world's volcanoes.

Forces of Nature. Creative Educational Society, 1971.

Captioned, color photographs of volcanoes, glaciers, tornadoes, earthquakes, and other natural phenomena present a useful overview of violent weather occurrences.

How Did We Find Out about Volcanoes? by Isaac Asimov. Walker, 1981.

Famous volcanoes through history and facts about volcanic action throughout the solar system answer the title's question.

Junior Science Book of Volcanoes, by Patricia Lauber. Garrard, 1965.

Chapters discuss lava; eruptions; and the causes, kinds, and structures of volcanoes.

Mount St. Helens: A Sleeping Volcano Awakes, by Marian T. Place. Dodd, 1981.

An overview of the events leading up to the recent disastrous eruption of Mount St. Helens in Washington is followed by some of the rescue and clean-up efforts.

This Restless Earth, by Patricia Lauber. Random, 1970.

Beginning with the formation of Surtsey Island off the coast of

Iceland, this book focuses on the many natural forces that shape and change the earth. The section on volcanoes includes an overview of some of the more well-known volcanoes and a discussion of the work of volcanologists.

Volcanoes, by Susan Harris. Watts, 1979.

Different types of eruptions and famous volcanoes are briefly discussed as is the concept of the geological plates that influence volcanic activity.

Volcanoes, by Ruth Radlauer. Childrens Pr., 1981.

Mount St. Helens is pictured as are Mount Hood, Katmai, and others.

Volcanoes: Nature's Fireworks, by Hershell H. Nixon and Joan L. Nixon. Dodd, 1978.

The study of volcanoes includes some of the benefits that can come from volcanic activity (such as using the heat from dormant volcanoes as a source of energy).

I Want a
Different Book

CURIOUS FACTS

Animal Fact/Animal Fable, by Seymour Simon. Crown, 1979.
Can some fish climb trees? It's a fact. Do cats have nine lives? It's a fable. Learn which is which from this amusing book.

The Biggest, Smallest, Fastest, Tallest Things You've Ever Heard Of,
by Robert Lopshire. Harper, 1980.
A funny book answers twenty-eight curious questions such as which song is sung more than any other. (It's "Happy Birthday to You.")

Encyclopedia Brown's Record Book of Weird and Wonderful Facts, by
Donald J. Sobol. Delacorte, 1979.
Encyclopedia Brown turns his talents from sleuthing to trivia and introduces all kinds of fascinating facts. There's a new record book (1981).

Factory Made: How Things Are Manufactured, by Leonard Gottlieb.
Houghton, 1978.
We may take buttons, baseballs, and toilet seats for granted; but this book tells you just how these and ten other everyday objects are made.

Guinness Book of Phenomenal Happenings, by Norris McWhirter
and Ross McWhirter. Sterling, 1976.
The unusual or unique, but true and accurate, happenings are one-to-a-page and are illustrated with black-and-white drawings. There is a short index.

The Improbable Book of Records, by Quentin Blake and John Yeoman. Atheneum, 1972.

Do you want to know the world's record time for balancing a banana on one's nose? Would you like to read about the boy with the most disgusting table manners or the world's strangest pet, a Fanged Beast from Planet X?

The Kids' Book of Lists, by Margo McLoone-Basta and Alice Siegel. Holt, 1980.

They were smart, brave, talented, or just happened to be there at the right time; but they were all under eighteen when they achieved the feats described in this book.

The Last Cow on the White House Lawn, by Barbara Seuling. Doubleday, 1978.

This trivia about the presidents, their wives, their children, and even their pets is not found in the history books.

Macmillan Illustrated Almanac for Kids, by Ann Elwood and others. Macmillan, 1981.

For lovers of almanacs here is one that gathers together things that you really want to know.

Stores, by Alvin Schwartz. Macmillan, 1977.

Ever wonder what goes on behind the scenes? From making spaghetti and meatballs for 200 people to mending shoes and cutting records, the author describes the activities of forty stores in his home town.

They Said It Couldn't Be Done, by Ross R. Olney. Dutton, 1979.

Build the Empire State Building or land on the moon? They said it couldn't be done, but these and other feats of science and engineering have been accomplished.

This Is the Way It Works: A Collection of Machines, by Robert Gardner. Doubleday, 1980.

From things as small as zippers to the loop-to-loop, this book tells you how they work.

You're Dumber in the Summer: And Over 100 Other Things No One Ever Told You, by Jim Aylward. Holt, 1980.

Did you know that the average mother in this country cooks 57,000 meals during her lifetime? Here are over 100 answers to questions you never thought you needed to know.

PUZZLERS

Anno's Britain, by Mitsumasa Anno. Philomel, 1982.

Follow a tiny wayfarer's journey across the countryside of Britain in a worldless travel book full of wonderfully detailed pictures.

Bet You Can't: Science Impossibilities to Fool You, by Vicki Cobb
and Kathy Darling. Lothrop, 1980.

Here are some tricks to fool your friends based on carefully explained scientific principles.

The Code and Cipher Book, by Jane Sarnoff and Reynold Ruffins.
Scribner, 1975.

Unravel the riddles of encoding and decoding messages in a wide variety of boggling, baffling, and bemusing codes, ciphers, and secret languages.

Codes, Ciphers and Secret Writing, by Martin Gardner. Simon &
Schuster, 1972.

Solve codes and ciphers with the help of these clear directions that begin with simple transposition and substitution ciphers and progress to the difficult polyalphabetic ones.

Fabulous Beasts, by Alison Lurie. Farrar, 1981.

Long ago travelers to remote parts of the world came back with tales of strange beasts such as the simurgh or the catoblepas. They are among the fantastic animals described in this book along with ones we know of today—the unicorn, the griffin, and the phoenix.

Fun with Pencil and Paper, by Joseph Leeming. Harper, 1955.

This variety of games, quizzes, and puzzles can be enjoyed with minimum equipment—pencil and paper.

The I Hate Mathematics! Book, by Marilyn Burns. Little, 1975.

Here is a lively collection of brain teasers for the mathematically disinclined as well as for those who do like mathematics!

Masquerade, by Kit Williams. Schocken, 1980.

Riddles and clues that are supposed to lead to a real treasure are contained in this story of love, adventures, fortunes lost, and a solid gold ornament.

The Mysterious Disappearance of Leon: (I Mean Noel), by Ellen Raskin. Dutton, 1971.

Word plays, name games, and mystery are all rolled up into a very funny search for a missing husband—the bride lost him when she was five and he was seven!

The Portmanteau Book, by Thomas Rockwell. Little, 1974.
"Portmanteau" means a large traveling bag or something with many qualities, and that's what this is—a perambulating grab bag of very funny stories, poems, a comic book, a maze, and the craziest cookbook ever, not to mention the index!

The Puzzle School, by Gerard Mosler. Harper, 1977.
A challenging but fun collection of quizzes, puzzles, and teasers is arranged in subject categories such as math, science, and social studies.

Solve It, by James F. Fixx. Doubleday, 1978.
A perplexing profusion of puzzles provides fun with some tricky solutions for puzzle fans.

Upside-Downers, More Pictures to Stretch the Imagination, by Mitsumasa Anno. Weatherhill, 1971.
Stairs are the best for going up or down in these creative 3-D pictures as well as in a real situation!

The Wagon Man, by Arthur Crowley. Houghton, 1981.
A mysterious man invites the children to come to Tarry Town where all they will do is play, and they all climb in the wagon. One boy eventually wants to leave, and the Wagon Man tells him that if he does not understand the riddle, he can never leave.

Weird and Wacky Inventions, by Jim Murphy. Crown, 1978.
Look at the picture of a strange invention, guess what it is, then turn the page and learn all about grapefruit shields, egg cleaners, used gum receptacles, and much more.

The Westing Game, by Ellen Raskin. Dutton, 1978.
Samuel Westing's will sets forth a challenging puzzle that his sixteen heirs must solve. The clues and word puzzles are all there for you, too.

What's Hatching Out of That Egg? by Patricia Lauber. Crown, 1979.
Enjoy a guessing game about the newborn creatures hatching from eleven different eggs through closeup photographs of the life cycles of the animals.

Where Are the Car Books?

Behind the Wheel, by Edward Koren. Holt, 1972.

The illustrations are of dashboards/instrument panels and views from behind the steering wheels of a car, truck, bus, speedboat, helicopter, crane, bulldozer, subway train, tractor, tugboat, airplane, and motorcycle.

Big Rigs, by Hope I. Marston. Dodd, 1980.

Clear photographs explain the various parts of the big eighteen-wheel diesel tractor trailers seen on today's highways. A guide to the different makes of diesels will help you pick out the different kinds.

Big Trucks, by the editors of *Consumer Guide.* Bell, 1977.

Arranged by manufacturer, the book covers the major truck producers, giving a short history of the companies and the types of trucks they produce. Color photos of the tractors are in a center section.

Classic Sports Cars, by Richard L. Knudson. Lerner, 1978.

Color photographs illustrate some of the classic European sports cars: the M.G., Jaguar, Bugatti, Mercedes-Benz, Porsche, and the American entry, the Corvette.

Monsters on Wheels, by George Ancona. Dutton, 1974.

The straddle crane and piggybacker are especially interesting, but many other big trucks from scraper to Lunar Rover are also detailed and illustrated with large photos.

The President's Car, by Nancy W. Parker. Crowell, 1981.

Each president makes a decision about the official car he will use, and this makes a variety of ways that presidents have been transported and protected. The current presidential car is a 1974 model that has been repainted.

Tin Lizzie, by Peter Spier. Doubleday, 1975.

The history of a Model T touring car is developed by following it through its various owners to restoration. Watercolor illustrations make this an especially lovely book, and details of the parts of a Model T are in the back.

Truck, by Donald Crews. Greenwillow, 1980.

One large red truck moves through other vehicles on the highway in different kinds of weather. The traffic signs and billboards provide the only words.

The Truck Book, by Robert L. Wolfe. Carolrhoda, 1981.

The variety of trucks shown here includes fire trucks, cement trucks, and garbage trucks. Photographs show both the entire truck and special details.

I Want Something
to Make Me Laugh

FUNNY STORIES

All the Money in the World, by Bill Brittain. Harper, 1979.
What would happen if a child really were given all the money in
the world? No one can foresee the complications.

Commander Toad in Space, by Jane Yolen. Coward, 1980.
The villainous Deep Wader menaces the intrepid crew of *Star
Warts;* but Commander Toad, Lieutenant Lily, and young Jake Skyjum-
per survive to go where no spaceship has gone before and take a bit
of earth out to the alien stars.

Fat Men from Space, by Daniel M. Pinkwater. Dodd, 1977.
A filling in William's tooth brings in a radio broadcast about space
people who have a wild craving for potato pancakes and are invad-
ing earth. William's built-in radio creates exhilarating moments at
school and at home. Boarding the spaceburger of the junk food
pirates, he narrowly escapes being carried along for a lifetime in
space.

Freaky Friday, by Mary Rodgers. Harper, 1972.
Annabel finds herself suddenly and inexplicably in her mother's
body. Can she act like her mother?

Freddy the Detective, by Walter R. Brooks. Knopf, 1932.
Freddy is a clever pig with great self-confidence. He organizes the
animals at Mr. Bean's farm (a place of many adventures) into a
sightseeing business and then into a detective bureau that advertises

"plain and fancy shadowing. Stolen articles restored. Criminals captured."

Half Magic, by Edward Eager. Harcourt, 1954.
Jane finds a nickel, and then some very unusual things begin to happen. When her mother borrows the nickel, she has some strange surprises, too.

Konrad, by Christine Nöstlinger. Watts, 1977.
One day a package is delivered to Mrs. Bertie Bartolotti. When she opens it up, she finds a factory-made and guaranteed-perfect seven-year-old boy named Konrad. Perfect Konrad's adventures help him turn into a normal, not-so-perfect boy.

The Lemonade Trick, by Scott Corbett. Little, 1960.
Kerby encounters strange Mrs. Graymalkin in the park and acquires from her a magic chemistry set. He finds a substance that turns good boys to bad and vice versa, and it even works on dogs!

McBroom Tells a Lie, by Sid Fleischman. Little, 1976.
McBroom is cheated by the villainous Mr. Heck in buying eighty acres of marshy pond. Eighty acres DEEP, it is. An unprecedented hot spell dries it up, and there is an acre of fabulously fertile soil; pumpkin vines grow so fast the kids try to catch a ride.

The Mushroom Center Disaster, by N. M. Bodecker. Atheneum, 1974.
When the remains of a human picnic come crashing down on this gentle insect community, the inhabitants turn disaster into triumph by ingeniouly making use of every bit of trash.

My Father's Dragon, by Ruth S. Gannett. Random, 1948.
A boy frees a baby dragon from captivity with the help of some chewing gum, a toothbrush and toothpaste, a comb and hairbrush, seven ribbons in assorted colors, two dozen pink lollipops, and six magnifying glasses.

Runaway Ralph, by Beverly Cleary. Morrow, 1970.
Seeking adventure, excitement, and medium-sized children who eat peanut butter and jelly sandwiches, Ralph, the daring mouse on a motorcycle, heads for summer camp.

The Shrinking of Treehorn, by Florence P. Heide. Holiday, 1971.
Treehorn finds himself becoming smaller and learns that everyone is too busy to care. He works out a solution after days of frustration

but discovers another big change. He decides not to say anything, figuring no one will notice.

RIDDLES AND JOKES

Ballpoint Bananas and Other Jokes for Children, by Charles Keller. Prentice-Hall, 1973.
   Jokes, riddles, and knock-knocks have their absurd answers, and the book also has some well-known and outlandish rhymes and illustrations.

CDB! by William Steig. Simon & Schuster, 1968.
   Instead of one-liners these jokes involve one letter: "CDB! DBSAB-ZB." The humorous pictures help you solve the messages.

Gunga, Your Din-Din Is Ready: Son of Puns, Gags, Quips and Riddles, by Roy Doty. Doubleday, 1976.
   "What is a polygon? A dead parrot." "What song did Count Dracula hate? 'Peg o' My Heart.' "

The Hodgepodge Book: An Almanac of American Folklore, collected by Duncan Emrich. Scholastic, 1972.
   Cures, knock-knock jokes, funny math games, taunts and teases, word games, riddles, and tongue twisters are "amusements" from American folklore.

I Know! A Riddle Book, by Jane Sarnoff and Reynold Ruffins. Scribner, 1976.
   Riddles of all kinds from the well-known "What does a 300-pound mouse say? Here, kitty, kitty kitty" to the just plain silly "What is green and makes holes? A drill pickle" will bring forth lots of giggles.

Knockout Knock Knocks, by Caroline A. Levine. Dutton, 1978.
   Doesn't everyone love knock-knock jokes?

Laugh Lines, by Charles Keller. Prentice-Hall, 1974.
   These are visual jokes you can tell with a paper and pencil. There are also some stories you can draw and tell that have surprise endings.

The Little Book of Fowl Jokes, by Warren Lyfick. Harvey House, 1980.

"What do they call a smart duck in school? A wise quacker" is one of the silly bird jokes in this book, which also includes ridiculous riddles.

107 3/4 Elephant Jokes, by Jack Stokes. Doubleday, 1979.

These hilarious elephant jokes may elicit groans as well as giggles: "How can you tell if an elephant used your toothbrush? It smells of peanuts."

Star-Spangled Banana: And Other Revolutionary Riddles, by Charles Keller and Richard Baker. Prentice-Hall, 1974.

American history does not have to be dull. "What did the American navy do when the British ships came at them as thick as peas? Shell them, of course."

Too Funny for Words: Gesture Jokes for Children, compiled by Charles Keller. Prentice-Hall, 1973.

These are jokes that have to be acted out to be appreciated. They are illustrated with black-and-white photographs.

Tyrannosaurus Wrecks, by Noelle Sterne. Harper, 1979.

A collection of dinosaur jokes, puns, and riddles includes: "Why didn't anyone want to sleep in the same room with Daddy dinosaur? Because he was a Bronto-snorus." "What do you call a dinosaur telephone? A rep-dial."

A Very Mice Joke Book, by Karen J. Gounaud. Houghton, 1981.

The jokes about mice ("What does Sherlock Mouse do for a living? He solves mouseteries") and the world they live in ("What four letter word do mice use when they get angry? RATS!") are rollicking fun.

Wags to Witches: More Jokes, Riddles, and Puns, by Victoria Gomez. Lothrop, 1981.

The clever word play in this collection of jokes and riddles ("Where do you park a coffee pot? In a perking lot") will make it a punster's favorite.

What? A Riddle Book, by Jane Sarnoff. Scribner, 1974.

Unusual illustrations make this book almost as much fun to look at as it is to read. An example of the riddles is: "What did Delaware? She wore her New Jersey."

SILLY POEMS

Amelia Mixed the Mustard and Other Poems, selected and illustrated by Evaline Ness. Scribner, 1975.
One of the twenty poems is:
>"Amelia mixed the mustard,
>She mixed it good and thick;
>She put it in the custard
>And made her Mother sick."

The Complete Nonsense Book, by Edward Lear. Dodd, 1961.
Both pictures and verse contain loads of laughter with "Queery Leary Nonsense," "Nonsense Cookery," "Nonsense Alphabets," "Laughable Lyrics," and now very famous limericks.

Custard and Company, by Ogden Nash. Little, 1980.
A perfectly funny combination of words and drawings is about celery, eels, wombats, panthers, mustard—and just about anything else.

Father Fox's Pennyrhymes, by Clyde Watson. Harper, 1971.
You might like to read about the goose:
>"Happy Birthday, Silly Goose!
>Just today we'll let you loose
>But if tomorrow you are hooked,
>Then my dear, your goose is cooked."

Garbage Delight, by Dennis Lee. Houghton, 1977.
These nonsense poems focus on meaningful topics such as getting stuck in a sweater, the miseries of sitting in a mud puddle, and worms.

I Met a Man, by John Ciardi. Houghton, 1961.
"I met a man in an onion bed./He was crying so hard his eyes were red."

Laughing Time: Nonsense Poems, by William J. Smith. Delacorte, 1980.
Do you know "A lady who lived in Uganda . . . was outrageously fond of her Panda"?

A Light in the Attic, by Shel Silverstein. Harper, 1981.
Come meet some of these funny friends—Memorizin Me, Ticklish

Tom, and the Polar Bear in the Frigidaire—that the author has found tucked away in his attic.

My Tang's Tungled and Other Ridiculous Situations, collected by Sara Brewton and others. Harper, 1973.
These tongue twisters, limericks, and nonsense poems are about flying fleas, eating peas, and buzzing bees.

Oh, Such Foolishness! poems selected by William Cole. Harper, 1978.
It's just silly willy-nilliness, dopey hillbilliness, rolling down the hilliness!

Poem Stew, poems selected by William Cole. Harper, 1981.
If you like to eat, you'll enjoy these poems about food.

The Queen of Eene, by Jack Prelutsky. Greenwillow, 1978.
The Queen of Eene rules this roost. And she brushes her teeth with onion juice.

Rolling Harvey down the Hill, by Jack Prelutsky. Greenwillow, 1980.
If you ever had a friend like Harvey, or maybe you do, you would never live it down. "Harvey's always showing off,/He wins when he competes,/It isn't that he's better,/It's that Harvey always cheats."

Where the Sidewalk Ends, by Shel Silverstein. Harper, 1974.
Where the sidewalk ends, you'll meet Skinny McGuinn, who disappears while taking a bath; Dirty Dan, the world's dirtiest man; Hector the Collector; and other absurd people.

I Want a Book
Where the Animals Talk

A Bear Called Paddington, by Michael Bond. Houghton, 1960.

Named after Paddington Station in London where the Brown family first meets him, the bear Paddington, from darkest Peru and very fond of marmalade, is soon settled with the family but unsettling to those who participate in his schemes.

The Bears Upstairs, by Dorothy Haas. Greenwillow, 1978.

Wendy first meets the bears, Otto and Ursula Ma'am, when they arrive early one rainy morning in a taxi. They have blue eyes and speak in soft furry voices. They are hiding in the upstairs apartment until their friends from the planet Brun come to get them. But will they come in time?

Bunnicula: A Rabbit-Tale of Mystery, by Deborah Howe and James Howe. Atheneum, 1979.

Chester the cat is sure the bunny Bunnicula (found at a Dracula movie) is a vampire when the Monroe family's vegetables mysteriously turn white. The dog Harold disagrees but writes the story of Chester's attempts to warn the family and rescue them.

The Days When the Animals Talked: Black American Folktales and How They Came to Be, by William J. Faulkner. Follett, 1977.

These twenty-seven folktales are retold by a folklorist who heard them first from Simon Brown, a former slave.

Dominic, by William Steig. Farrar, 1972.

Dominic's carefree dog philosophy about trouble keeps entangling him with the vicious Doomsday Gang.

Harry Cat's Pet Puppy, by George Selden. Farrar, 1974.

Harry Cat and Tucker Mouse salvage a stray puppy in New York. However, he eats too much, grows too big for their drainpipe home, and is generally untrained; so Harry and Tucker set out to find a suitable home for him.

Impossible Possum, by Ellen Conford. Little, 1971.

Until his sister tricks him, Randolph the possum thinks it is impossible for him to hang by his tail.

Mother Crocodile: An Uncle Amadou Tale from Senegal, by Rosa Guy. Delacorte, 1981.

When little crocodiles close their ears to old but true tales, they may pay dearly. Dia, the mother crocodile, hears enough to direct them out of trouble when war starts.

Rabbit Hill, by Robert Lawson. Viking, 1944.

Georgie and his family and the other animals on Rabbit Hill are very much interested in the new folks who are moving in. Will they be friends or enemies?

The Rescuers, by Margery Sharp. Little, 1959.

A white mouse, Miss Bianca, who lives in luxury in the Embassy's schoolroom, and Bernard, a more common mouse from the pantry, set out on a rescue mission to save a poet imprisoned in the Black Castle.

A Story, A Story, an African Tale, by Gail E. Haley. Atheneum, 1970.

Ananse, the "Spider Man," fulfills his three-part bargain with Nayame the Sky God and secures the right to tell stories.

A Toad for Tuesday, by Russell Erickson. Lothrop, 1974.

Warton should not have gone to visit Aunt Toolia in the middle of winter when all sensible toads are safe at home. He wishes he had listened to his brother Morton when he is captured by an owl who plans to eat him for Tuesday dinner.

Where Are the
Books about the War?

HOLOCAUST

Anne Frank: The Diary of a Young Girl. Doubleday, 1952.
This famous true diary deals with the Nazi persecution of the Jews in the 1930s and 1940s, now known as the Holocaust.

The Borrowed House, by Hilda Van Stockum. Farrar, 1975.
Twelve-year-old Janna, a former member of a Hitler youth group, rejoins her theatrical family in a rented Dutch house. She wonders why the owners left all their possessions and learns the truth from the Jewish Dutch boy she finds hiding in the attic.

Brother Enemy, by Elisabeth Mace. Beaufort, 1981.
Andreas, a seven-year-old German, discovers he is part Jewish when he is sent to live in prewar England with his refugee father. He lives with British families and is reunited at fifteen with his Aryan half brother.

The Devil in Vienna, by Doris Orgel. Dial, 1978.
Though Inge is Jewish and Liselotte is from a Nazi family, they are best friends in Vienna in 1938. As related in his diary, their dangerous friendship continues through secret meetings until Inge's family escapes to Yugoslavia.

The Endless Steppe, by Esther Hautzig. Harper, 1968.
In June of 1941, the Rudomin family was arrested in Yilna, Poland, and sent with other "capitalists" in a crowded railroad car to Siberia. Without bitterness Esther Rudomin, who was ten years old at the time, writes about the five years of hardship for this Jewish family.

Friedrich, by Hans P. Richter. Holt, 1970.

The young German narrator traces his growing awareness of Jewish persecution through the life of Friedrich, his friend from babyhood. Short chapters advance the story from 1925 to 1942 when Friedrich is killed in a bombing raid because he is refused shelter as a Jew.

I Never Saw Another Butterfly: Children's Drawings and Poems from Theresienstadt Concentration Camp, 1942–1944. McGraw-Hill, 1964.

All that is left of these children are their drawings, reproduced here in color, and their touching poems on their hopes, fears, and the world around them in the ghetto and concentration camp.

Never to Forget: The Jews of the Holocaust, by Milton Meltzer. Harper, 1976.

Many incidents of the German destruction of Jews are included in an overview of that time, using quotations from personal diaries and similar reportage.

A Pocket Full of Seeds, by Marilyn Sachs. Doubleday, 1973.

Nicole Nieman, protected from the Nazis in her French boarding school, looks back over the events that changed her Jewish childhood and broke up her average, happy family.

The Secret Ship, by Ruth Kluger and Peggy Mann. Doubleday, 1978.

A secret agent of the Mossad smuggles Jewish refugees onto an illegal ship bound for Palestine in 1939, the largest secret rescue movement of all time.

Till the Break of Day, by Maia Wojciechowska. Harcourt, 1972.

Maia's family escapes from Poland after the 1939 German invasion to France, and later to America, when she is a teenager.

Upon the Head of the Goat, by Aranka Siegal. Farrar, 1981.

Slowly but insidiously, restrictions and cruelties are perpetuated on the Jewish people in Hungary during World War II. The Davidowitz family are put on a train by German soldiers without any possessions and sent to Auschwitz concentration camp.

The Upstairs Room, by Johanna Reiss. Harper, 1972.

Separated from her mother, father, and sister, the Jewish author vividly recalls her day-to-day experiences with another sister while hidden in an upstairs room of a remote Dutch farmhouse where they are cared for by a very human Gentile family.

When Hitler Stole Pink Rabbit, by Judith Kerr. Coward, 1971.
Forced to flee Germany with her family when anti-Semitism becomes very strong, Anna leaves behind a stuffed rabbit, which, as they move from country to country, makes her realize that they have left for good.

WORLD WAR II

Adolf Hitler, a Portrait in Tyranny, by Edward F. Dolan, Jr. Dodd, 1981.
This biography of Hitler is complete from his birth to death and there is a center section of photographs. It is a rather full account of the war years in which the author attributes the cruelties in the concentration camps to a contagious madness and the extension of the war into Poland to German pride.

Air War against Hitler's Germany, by Stephen W. Sears. American Heritage, 1964.
Major events of the Allied attacks on Germany are outlined. Many color and black-and-white photos illustrate this attractive volume.

An Album of World War II, by Dorothy Hoobler and Thomas Hoobler. Watts, 1977.
Many realistic photographs, maps, and a clear text follow the course of the war from the rise of Fascism through the defeat of Japan. War is not glamorized in the pictures that show tragedy and death on both sides.

The Ark, by Margot Benary-Isbert. Harcourt, 1953.
Margaret and her family wander from camp to camp after World War II in search of a home and work until, in West Germany, they find a farm and the Ark.

The Battle of Britain, by Quentin Reynolds. Random, 1953.
This battle lasted eighty-four days in 1940; and much of it was an air battle between the German Luftwaffe and the RAF, the British Royal Air Force. The British people fought the fires set off by the bombs and never gave up; they took Hitler's hardest punch.

Carrie's War, by Nina Bawden. Harper, 1973.

Carrie and her brother are removed to Wales for safety from the bombings in World War II; there they meet a variety of people, some sympathetic, some harsh, some mysterious. In a flashback plot we first meet adult Carrie haunted by a tragedy she believes she caused during that time.

A Child in Prison Camp, by Shizuye Takashima. Morrow, 1974.

For no reason but its ancestry, a Canadian-Japanese family is imprisoned during World War II and held in one of the detention camps operated in the United States and Canada.

The Cigarette Sellers of Three Crosses Square, by Joseph Ziemian. Lerner, 1975.

Without parents, without homes, without proper identification papers, Conky, Bull, Toothy, Teresa, and other Jewish children in Warsaw dodge the Gestapo in 1944 and sell cigarettes and newspapers in order to survive.

The First Book of World War II, by Louis Snyder. Watts, 1958.

This history outlines the politics and military operations of World War II and includes black-and-white photos and maps to illustrate the action.

Hiroshima No Pika, by Toshi Maruki. Lothrop, 1980.

Mii and her mother survive the Flash, the atomic bomb that fell on Hiroshima at 8:15 on the morning of August 6, 1945; and Mii, seven at the time and still the same size now, places a lighted lantern adrift on the river every year in a ceremony in memory of her father and others who died that day.

I Was There, by Hans P. Richter. Holt, 1972.

Three boys who belong to the Hitler youth movement participate in simple activities such as collecting iron and then taking premilitary training. Their friendship and differing feelings are described before two of them are killed in the war.

The Machine Gunners, by Robert Westall. Greenwillow, 1975.

When a group of English children discover a German machine gun in a downed airplane, they prepare to use it against an expected enemy invasion.

The Rise and Fall of Adolf Hitler, by William L. Shirer. Random, 1961.

In almost equal parts, four main topics are covered: the early years of Adolf Hitler, his rise to power, World War II, and the collapse of Germany, ending with his death.

Seabees of World War II, by Edmund L. Castillo. Random, 1963.
What the Seabees did during World War II is shown in photographs and descriptions of battlefront operations.

Snow Treasure, by Marie McSwigan. Dutton, 1942.
A group of Norwegian children hurtle on their sleds down a mountain, straight through the camp of the Nazi occupation forces, hiding blocks of gold they are helping to remove from the country.

The Story of D-Day, by R. Conrad Stein. Childrens Pr., 1977.
On D-Day, June 6, 1944, the main site for battle was the northern coast of France, and the weather report was for only one good day of calm seas for the over 4000 boats that were carrying 155,000 Allied soldiers to the beaches.

The Story of World War II, by Stewart Graff. Dutton, 1978.
Basically, a terse, accurately illustrated chronology, the book covers the land and sea battles on the Russian, Pacific, and North African fronts.

The Story of World War II, by Robert Leckie. Random, 1964.
This comprehensive account of the entire war gives depth to understanding its events.

The Supercarriers, by George Sullivan. Dodd, 1980.
How the aircraft carriers of the U.S. Navy work and the role of these ships in World War II battles are described.

World War II Aircraft in Combat, by Glenn B. Bavousett. Arco, 1976.
More than forty World War II aircraft are accurately shown in action paintings. Although not a total picture of the air war, this is a partial record of its progress, each plane's part, and the several theaters of action.

World War Two, an Illustrated History in Colour, 1939–1945, by Robert Hoare, edited by R. J. Unstead. Macdonald Educational, 1973.
Hundreds of photographs and sketches illustrate this breakdown of the war into approximately twenty-five topics, with two pages of text and pictures for each one. Virtually every aspect of World War

II from a British viewpoint is included; and there are about twelve pages of who's who, war poems and songs, directions for plotting World War II battles in a reference section, plus an index.

I Want a
Halloween Story

The Blue-Nosed Witch, by Margaret Embry. Holiday, 1956.

Blanche, a real witch although a young one, has a nose that glows a wonderful blue in the dark. One Halloween night while flying on her broomstick with her black cat, she sees a group of children trick-or-treating, and she flies down to join them.

Dorrie and the Halloween Plot, by Patricia Coombs. Lothrop, 1976.

While practicing flying on a big broomstick (in her mother's absence), Dorrie overhears the Halloween Demons plotting and manages to save some magic recipes.

The Hairy Horror Trick, by Scott Corbett. Little, 1969.

When their planned experiment with Kerby's Feats O'Magic Chemistry Set goes awry, Kerby and Fenton find themselves in possession of a beard, a mustache, and a hairless dog. They spend Halloween evening trying to frighten themselves and scare the hair off their faces.

Halloween Cookbook, by Susan Purdy. Watts, 1977.

Sections on equipment, ingredients, substitutions, measuring, safety, and basic cooking skills precede the thirty-one recipes, which are well-illustrated and easy to follow. Although about half are desserts, vegetables, main dishes, and edible decorations are also included.

Hey-How for Halloween, edited by Lee B. Hopkins. Harcourt, 1974.

The majority of these poems are directly related to Halloween and are not simply ghost or witch poems. Several white-on-black illustrations produce a nice effect.

In the Witch's Kitchen, compiled by John E. Brewton and others. Harper, 1980.

The illustrations are humorous, as are most of the poems, in this collection about witches, spooks, and a favorite holiday, Halloween.

It's Halloween, by Jack Prelutsky. Greenwillow, 1977.

These thirteen poems with buoyant pictures are definitely funny rather than scary.

Jenny's Moonlight Adventure, by Esther Averill. Harper, 1949.

The little black cat Jenny braves the dogs of Mulligan Street to return a flute to the injured Madame Butterfly.

Little Witch, by Anna E. Bennett. Harper, 1953.

Minikin Snickasnee is the pivot of a plot involving the ordinary children she longs to have as friends and her disagreeable mother who has the unfortunate practice of turning the children into flowerpots.

No More Magic, by Avi. Pantheon, 1975.

When his bicycle disappears on Halloween night, Chris believes magic is involved. His bike, though old, has always seemed somehow special, almost magical to him. Chris thinks other strange happenings may be connected: Muffin's warlock costume being stolen, someone wearing it trick-or-treating at Chris's house only, and Muffin's parents being missing.

The Spook Book, by Burton Marks and Rita Marks. Lothrop, 1981.

Surprise your friends with ideas on games, treats, and costumes for the best Halloween fun in the neighborhood.

Witch Poems, edited by Daisy Wallace. Holiday, 1976.

You will pore over the humorous and chilling poems and the creepy details of the black-and-white drawings.

I Like Sports.
Do You Have a Book
about . . .?

BASEBALL

The Ballpark: One Day behind the Scenes of a Major League Game,
 by William Jaspersohn. Little, 1980.
 A behind-the-scenes look at Fenway Park, home of the Boston Red
Sox, is profusely illustrated with large, appealing photographs and
gives an inside look at what happens before, during, and after games.

Baseball Fever, by Johanna Hurwitz. Morrow, 1981.
 Ezra is a Mets fan who at ten years of age has a fine memory for
baseball facts, but he also has to use his mind to learn to play chess
with his father before he can get his father to appreciate baseball.

Baseball for Young Champions, by Robert J. Antonacci. McGraw-
 Hill, 1977.
 How to play each position, how to train properly, the history of
baseball, and the tools of the ballplayer are included along with
practical information such as how to figure batting averages and
practice drills.

Baseball Is for Me, by Lowell A. Dickmeyer. Lerner, 1978.
 A boy in his first year of little league play takes a look at some of
the realities of the game (sitting on the bench) and baseball terms.

The Goof That Won the Pennant, by Jonah Kalb. Houghton, 1976.
 The Blazers are a hopeless baseball team. Each season they place
last with a typical score being Cubs 14–Blazers 0. With the new
season Coach Veniti has a motto, "winning is always more fun than
losing"; but the team has an uphill fight to gain confidence.

Hang Tough, Paul Mather, by Alfred Slote. Lippincott, 1973.

Paul loves to play baseball and is a good pitcher. When his parents find out he has leukemia, they insist that he stop playing; but Paul sneaks off to play and lands up back in the hospital.

Here Comes the Strikeout, by Leonard Kessler. Harper, 1965.

Bobby did very well at running the bases, sliding, and catching balls; but he could not hit the ball. With the help of a friend, Bobby begins to improve; and practice helps in the long run.

The Home Run Trick, by Scott Corbett. Little, 1973.

The Panthers think they have made a great deal when they agree to have the winner of the Panther-Wildcat baseball game receive new equipment if the winner plays a game against the Taylorville Toms. The only catch is that the Toms are girls. The team turns to a magic chemistry set for assistance.

How to Play Better Baseball, by C. Paul Jackson. Harper, 1963.

Playing positions, equipment, hitting, base running, and strategy are covered; and the requirements of each player on the team are analyzed.

Matt Gargan's Boy, by Alfred Slote. Lippincott, 1975.

Danny Gargan, son of a professional baseball player, loves baseball. He wants his divorced parents to get back together, but instead his mother goes out with Herb, whose daughter is the first girl to try out for Danny's team.

Play Ball, Amelia Bedelia, by Peggy Parish. Harper, 1972.

When asked to fill in for a sick player on a baseball team, Amelia Bedelia does. Since Amelia Bedelia always takes words literally, when told to tag Jack, she gets a price tag and puts it on him.

Thank You, Jackie Robinson, by Barbara Cohen. Lothrop, 1974.

Sam is crazy about baseball, particularly the Brooklyn Dodgers. He develops a strong friendship with an older black man when he realizes that they both are big Dodger fans.

Warm Up for Little League Baseball, by Morris Shirts. Sterling, 1976.

Good advice, tips, and strategy on pitching, throwing, catching, baserunning, and fielding emphasize boys and girls playing together. The photographs are full of action and stress good technique.

SOCCER

Better Soccer for Boys and Girls, by George Sullivan. Dodd, 1978.
Action photographs explain and demonstrate the positions, skills, and exercises for soccer. The author also includes diagrams and explanations of some tactical formations and ten problems to solve about soccer rules.

The Great Game of Soccer, by Howard Liss. Putnam, 1979.
Soccer skills and positions are briefly described and demonstrated by photos of children five years and older learning to play. Also included are the history of the game and pictures and information about Pelé and other international superstars.

Gunnar Scores a Goal, by Kerstin Thorvall. Harcourt, 1968.
Nine-year-old Gunnar's older brothers always tease him until he begins playing some good soccer games on a new friend's team. He and the soccer ball work well together!

Hawkins and the Soccer Solution, by Barbara B. Wallace. Abingdon, 1981.
A bit of crazy chaos, an out-of-place English butler, and a team with a string of problems (no sponsor, no coach, no money, and an excess of "left feet") limit the play-by-play action, but sportsmanship is the goal.

How to Play Better Soccer, by C. Paul Jackson. Harper, 1978.
A brief history of soccer is followed by a thorough explanation of the game, the field, position play, equipment, practices, exercises, and official signals. All of this is well-illustrated with diagrams and humorous drawings showing boys and girls participating.

Illustrated Soccer Dictionary for Young People, by James B. Gardner. Harvey House, 1976.
Almost 250 soccer terms are listed in alphabetical order and explained. Most of the words and expressions are also described with very amusing drawings of soccer players in action. Brief summaries are given of superstars Pelé, Kyle Rote, Jr., Stanley Matthews, and Eusebio de Silva Ferreira.

Jackrabbit Goalie, by Matt Christopher. Little, 1978.
Pepper stretches the truth, not once, but twice! He wants to play soccer and pretends to be a goalie when he really is not, but he works so hard with the team that he helps win games.

Soccer for Young Champions, by Robert J. Antonacci. McGraw-Hill, 1978.

The history and the development of soccer are accompanied by complete explanations of how to play the game with clear drawings of boys and girls demonstrating plays. Rules, playing field sizes for various ages, scorekeeping, and records are covered as well as the participation in and enjoyment of soccer by nonplayers.

Soccer Halfback, by Matt Christopher. Little, 1978.

Jabber loves soccer but is being pressured by his family to play football.

Soccer Hero, by Mike Neigoff. Albert Whitman, 1976.

Specs, the greatest organizer and manager in junior high, but also the shortest and least athletic, talks up a soccer team. Starting with nothing, he gets together a team, a coach, goals, and a field. Then Specs wants to play, not just manage.

Soccer Is for Me, by Lowell A. Dickmeyer. Lerner, 1978.

Todd, a young soccer player, tells about his experiences with his teammates, the Dolphins. With photos of the young players in action he tells in his own words about the games, the practicing of drills and skills, and his hope of becoming a goalkeeper.

The Soccer Orphans, by William MacKellar. Dodd, 1979.

Since Jamie is too short and lightweight to make the football team in his new hometown where games must be won at any cost, he and others rejected for football develop a soccer team. Obstacles like prejudice and lack of support just build their toughness and sportsmanship.

Starting Soccer: A Handbook for Boys and Girls, by Edward F. Dolan, Jr. Harper, 1976.

Techniques and strategies are detailed and can be difficult to follow so the photographs of boys and girls demonstrating plays are extremely helpful.

You Can Control the Soccer Ball! by Paul Harris with Adrian Walsh. Soccer for Americans, 1977.

How to win control of the ball by concentration, exercise, and practice is shown in this little book of secrets by the world champion from Ireland, Adrian Walsh. There are many clear photos demonstrating juggling, flexibility, and balance and also a section on equipment and how to care for it.

The World's #1 Best Selling Soccer Book, by Ken Laitin and Steve Laitin. Messner, 1979.

The motivation for playing soccer, the players, skills, and problems are explored in their very personal approach. Throughout are excellent photos explaining the text and also funny drawings and sayings by the authors, two teenage brothers who wrote this from their experiences after playing soccer since they were seven.

SURFING

Better Surfing for Boys, by Joseph J. Cook and William R. Romeika. Dodd, 1967.

The beginner is shown how to carry a board and how to catch a wave, and a twelve-photo-sequence demonstrates how to stand upright on a board. Brief sections on hot-dogging, body surfing, belly-boarding, and even skateboarding end the book.

Broderick, by Edward Ormondroyd. Parnassus, 1969.

Inspired by a book he happens to be chewing, Broderick, a mouse, makes a board from a tongue depressor and practices until he masters the waves. The intrepid mouse with sunbleached fur finds fame and fortune as a surfer.

Kings of the Surf, by Ross R. Olney and Richard W. Graham. Putnam, 1969.

Surfers are a varied breed, some noted for flashy maneuvers, others for a classic, graceful style, and still others for mastering towering waves. Here are twenty who have contributed to shaping the sport into what it is today. Wave riders from the East Coast, California, Hawaii, and Australia are represented.

Surf-Riding, by H. Arthur Klein. Harper, 1972.

Men and women surfers are shown on bellyboards, body surfing, standing on full-sized boards, or even riding tandem over the waves.

The Surfer's Almanac: An International Surfing Guide, by Gary F. R. Filosa. Dutton, 1977.

A map lists thirty-five surfsites around the world while the text describes surfing in countries from Australia to West Germany. The emphasis is on the United States, describing sites along the Great Lakes and in Arizona as well as those along the Pacific, Atlantic, and Gulf coasts. There is also a list of surfing organizations.

Surfing, Basic Techniques, by Arnold Madison. McKay, 1979.

A short instruction book for the beginning surfer emphasizes safety by starting with swimming skills recommended for the would-be surfer and ending with the surfing rules of conduct. Cartoons of the Silly Surfer demonstrate what happens when you ignore safety rules.

What Do You Have about Computers?

Computers, by Brian R. Smith. Usborne Electronics World, n.d.
Profusely illustrated in a cartoonish way, this book covers the history, types, languages, uses, and future prospects of computers.

The Creative Kid's Guide to Home Computers, by Fred D'Ignazio. Doubleday, 1981.
Imaginative projects on a variety of programmable home computers are suggested, and expert advice on selecting the right electronic device is given.

Katie and the Computer, by Fred D'Ignazio. Creative Computing Pr., 1979.
Her father introduces Katie to the language and abilities of a computer through a fairy-tale-style story.

My Computer Picture Dictionary, by Jean Rice and Marian Haley. Denison, 1981.
A good illustrated reference book for the young and the not-so-young.

The Revolt of 10-X, by Joan D. Carris. Harper, 1980.
Twelve-year-old Taylor has trouble coping with her father's sudden death. She spends most of her time working with the computer that she and her father had built. She programs it to control the power in her new house, to act as a mother to her pet gosling, and to complete her father's last gift to her mother.

I Want a Book Where the Story Happened a Long Time Ago

BIBLE STORIES

Bible Stories You Can't Forget, by Marshall Efron and Alfa-Betty Olsen. Dutton, 1976.

Not irreverent, this is a lighter view of human foibles of Biblical characters.

Every Man Heart Lay Down, by Lorenz Graham. Crowell, 1970.

This Liberian way of telling the Christmas story is refreshingly personal. The coming of the child Jesus is told as a beautiful song-poem, as understood by a modern African child.

Jonah: An Old Testament Story, by Beverly Brodsky. Harper, 1977.

Jonah tells us briefly, without detail, the basic facts of *all* his adventures, not just the one with the whale, when obeying God's command to warn Ninevah of its sins.

The Mighty Ones: Great Men and Women of Early Bible Days, by Meindert DeJong. Harper, 1959.

The founding of Israel in early Biblical days is retold in contemporary style through the lives of great men and women.

Noah's Ark, illustrated by Peter Spier. Doubleday, 1977.

The Dutch poem "The Flood" by Jacob Revius precedes the picturing of the Biblical story. The illustrations are full of humor but not irreverent as they picture the work of caring for the animals on the Ark, which increases day by day.

Shadrach, Meschach and Abednego, illustrated by Paul Galdone. McGraw-Hill, 1965.

Three young men defy the order of a powerful king, at the risk of death, in order to honor their faith in their God.

Stories from the Bible, by Walter De La Mare. Knopf, 1961.

Only Old Testament stories are included such as: The Garden of Eden, the Flood, Joseph, Moses, the Wilderness, Samson, Samuel, Saul, and David.

The Story of Christmas, illustrated by Felix Hoffmann. Atheneum, 1975.

The Biblical story of the birth of Jesus, from the angel's announcement to Mary until the child and his parents return to Nazareth in safety, is told by full-page pictures in which the people show their feelings about what happened.

Story of Jesus, illustrated by Maud Petersham and Miska Petersham. Macmillan, 1967.

The Petershams have illustrated a text selected directly from the King James version of the Bible with color and black-and-white drawings.

Taizé Picture Bible, illustrated by Brother Eric De Saussure. Fortress, 1969.

Stories from the Old and New Testaments are nicely adapted from the Jerusalem Bible and have the book and chapter source listed.

The Tall Book of Bible Stories, by Katherine Gibson. Harper, 1980.

Only the major stories—fifteen from the Old Testament and eleven from the New Testament—are told, but they are told with sufficient length and a minimal simplification of language.

CIVIL WAR

Across Five Aprils, by Irene Hunt. Follett, 1964.

Jethro Creighton is left on their farm in Illinois while his brothers go off to fight in the Civil War—one as a Union soldier, one as a Confederate.

I Want My Sunday, Stranger! by Patricia Beatty. Morrow, 1977.

Andrew Lancy, a Mormon boy from California, goes east, searching for his horse, which was taken by a Confederate soldier, and ends his quest at the Battle of Gettysburg.

Ironclad! A True Story of the Civil War, by Seymour Reit. Dodd, 1977.
The historic sea battle between the North's iron ship, the *Monitor*, and the South's *Merrimac* is seen through the eyes of a young crew member of the *Monitor*.

Jed, by Peter Burchard. Coward, 1960.
When he encounters a Southern boy with a broken leg, the young Yankee soldier Jed takes him home although he risks discovery from his inflexible captain.

Me and Willie and Pa, by F. N. Monjo. Simon & Schuster, 1973.
Tad Lincoln tells of the Civil War years in the White House with his father, the president.

The Perilous Road, by William O. Steele. Harcourt, 1958.
Chris, a Yankee-hating Tennessee mountain boy, learns by experience the futility of war when his spy report to the Confederates threatens his brother's life as he serves in the Union army.

Runaway Balloon: The Last Flight of Confederate Air Force One, by Burke Davis. Coward, 1976.
An actual Civil War incident involving Confederate soldier John Randolph Bryan's two flights in a balloon are humorously portrayed.

Thunder at Gettysburg, by Patricia L. Gauch. Coward, 1975.
As a resident of Gettysburg, young Tillie Pierce is swept into the midst of the battle between the Blues and the Grays that raged for three terrible days in July of 1863.

The Vicksburg Veteran, by F. N. Monjo. Simon & Schuster, 1971.
Fred Grant, thirteen, tells about the Vicksburg campaign as he experiences it with his famous father, General Ulysses S. Grant.

Zoar Blue, by Janet Hickman. Macmillan, 1978.
The Civil War brings turbulence and changes to two young people who live in the German Separatist settlement of Zoar, Ohio.

KNIGHTS AND CASTLES

Adam of the Road, by Elizabeth Janet Gray. Viking, 1942.

Roger tells his son Adam that the road is home to a minstrel. When they are separated from each other while looking for their stolen spaniel Nick, Adam travels to Oxford, Winchester, and London before he is reunited with his father and his dog and knows for sure he, too, wants the life of a minstrel "on the road."

The Art and Industry of Sandcastles, Being an Illustrated Guide to Basic Constructions along with Divers Information, devised by One Jan Adkins, a Wily Fellow. Walker, 1971.

To build a sandcastle like a real castle, you need to know a lot about castles and knights, which the author tells you with a mingling of how-to-work-with-sand pictures and others of famous castles and the people who lived and worked in them.

Castle, by David Macaulay. Houghton, 1977.

Thirteenth-century architecture was complicated and purposeful, and Macaulay includes a floor plan and pictures of laborers and tools to show the planning and construction from the time the site is selected until the finished castle is defended against invaders.

Children of the Red King, by Madeleine Polland. Holt, 1959.

In the middle of an Irish civil war the brave Princess Grania and her brother, the chosen heir to the throne, are captured by Norman invaders who hold them hostage in a castle.

Cowardly Clyde, by Bill Peet. Houghton, 1979.

Cowardly Clyde is the steed belonging to Sir Galavant. Together they try to get rid of a huge ogre who is a menace to the farmers round about. Clyde, although really not very brave, is the hero and is instrumental in making Sir Galavant look good—like a knight should.

The Door in the Wall, by Marguerite de Angeli. Doubleday, 1949.

Robin, the son of noble parents, must give up his dream of becoming a knight; but he proves his courage when he escapes a besieged castle and brings help.

Greta the Strong, by Donald J. Sobol. Follett, 1970.

After defeating her brothers in the knightly arts of chivalry, Greta proves her right to go on the quest for the sword Excalibur.

Half Magic, by Edward Eager. Harcourt, 1954.

Using a half-magic coin and simple arithmetic, Katharine transports herself to King Arthur's Court where she jousts with Sir Lancelot.

Harald and the Giant Knight, by Donald Carrick. Houghton, 1982.

Harald does not like having knights jousting on his family's farm. His father comes up with a plan to scare the plundering knights away, and Harald helps by collapsing their tents.

The Knight and the Dragon, by Tomie de Paola. Putnam, 1980.

Who is the more powerful, the knight or the dragon? Each one is insecure about the upcoming fight.

The Knight of the Lion, by Gerald McDermott. Scholastic, 1979.

Sir Yvain is a member of the king's court, and it is he who decides to conquer the Black Knight and capture the Fountain of Life.

Knight's Castle, by Edward Eager. Harcourt, 1956.

A battered toy soldier leads Roger back into the days of Ivanhoe and Robin Hood where he takes part in the siege of Torquilstone.

Knights in Armor, by Shirley Glubok. Harper, 1969.

Large, clear photographs of a wide variety of armor for both men and horses highlight a brief explanation of the uses of armor in the Middle Ages.

Living in a Castle, by R. J. Unstead. Addison-Wesley, 1973.

People-power, some 100 strong, ran the castles in contrast to our electrical appliances today. This book centers on a castle around 1250 and what the people ate and drank, how they spent their day, their manners and clothes, and their work and play.

The Maude Reed Tale, by Norah Lofts. Nelson, 1971.

Spending two years away from home to become a lady when she wants to be a wool merchant like her grandfather seems foolish to Maude at the age of twelve. However, knowing how to read and write helps her regain the business from a thieving manager.

The Sword in the Tree, by Clyde R. Bulla. Harper, 1956.

Shan, son of Lord Weldon, finds a hollow oak tree to house the sword he feels is rightly his.

MYTHS

Daedalus and Icarus, by Penelope Farmer. Harcourt, 1971.

Ordered to build an underground maze, the labyrinth, for the king of Crete, the engineer Daedulus proves his skill but later is imprisoned when the maze is breached. To escape, Daedalus plans an even greater feat, using feathers to prepare wings for his son Icarus and himself.

A Fair Wind for Troy, by Doris Gates. Viking, 1976.

The suitors of the beautiful Helen, daughter of Sparta's king Tyndareus, take an oath that later leads to the seige of the city of Troy.

The Golden God: Apollo, by Doris Gates. Viking, 1973.

Apollo is victorious over the serpent Python and hopelessly in love with Daphne. He is unlucky in his loves, but his greatest grief is the death of his son Phaethon, who could not control the horses that drew the chariot of the sun.

The Gorgon's Head, a Myth from the Isles of Greece, retold by Margaret Hodges. Little, 1972.

When Perseus is born and his death is foretold, he and his mother are put in a box and thrown into the sea; but they do not drown. Perseus, now a young man, must appease the gods and bring back the fearsome head of Medusa.

Lord of the Sky: Zeus, by Doris Gates. Viking, 1972.

The Greek god Zeus was also called All-High because he was powerful, and no mortal had ever penetrated the heights where he lived. He was also moody and romantic, which makes his life interesting and dangerous as he fights battles in his quests.

Norse God and Giants, by Ingri d'Aulaire and Edgar Parin d'Aulaire. Doubleday, 1967.

The Norse legends, written down by the Icelandic people, tell of the Frost Giants; Thor, the thunder-god, for whom Thursday is named; Odin, the raven god; and Skade, the ski goddess.

Pegasus, by Krystyna Turska. Watts, 1970.

In the city of Corinth there is a young man named Bellerophon who wishes to own the winged horse Pegasus for himself. When he does, they live many years together until Bellerophon, through his greed, is killed.

The Story of Persephone, by Penelope Farmer. Morrow, 1973.

Persephone, daughter of Demeter, the corn goddess, is kidnapped by Hades, god of the underworld. When Demeter's grief makes the earth barren, Zeus must intervene.

PIONEERS

The Cabin Faced West, by Jean Fritz. Coward, 1958.

Ann Hamilton is a lonely pioneer girl whose new friends include a settler whom she teaches to read, and George Washington, who happens to be passing by.

Caddie Woodlawn, by Carol R. Brink. Macmillan, 1973.

Caddie is a lively girl who lives in Wisconsin in the 1860s. With her brothers she befriends the Indians and a circuit rider. Later the family faces a decision about leaving the frontier.

Children of the Covered Wagon, by Mary J. Carr. Harper, 1957.

Jerry, Jim, and Myra share the dangers and adventures of a 2000-mile covered-wagon trip to Oregon in 1844. They struggle against the weather and struggle for food, meet Indians, ford raging rivers, and enjoy the campfires.

The Courage of Sarah Noble, by Alice Dalgliesh. Scribner, 1954.

Sarah is only eight, but she is big enough to go pioneering with her father and take care of him until others in the family join them. "Keep up your courage, Sarah Noble," says her mother as she wraps her own red-brown cloak around her daughter.

The Golden Venture, by Jane Flory. Houghton, 1976.

Minnie stows away on her father's wagon heading west from Missouri to join the California Gold Rush. While he is looking for gold, she encounters adventures of her own in San Francisco.

The Legend of New Amsterdam, by Peter Spier. Doubleday, 1979.

A lively excursion into early America to visit the settlers of what is now New York has the author-artist's pictures as a guide.

Mary Jemison: Seneca Captive, by Jeanne L. Gardner. Harcourt, 1966.

In 1758 the Seneca Indians raided a pioneer cabin, scalped the parents, and captured the young daughter Mary Jemison, whom they adopted as their own. This is the true story of how Mary learned Indian skills and chose to live with the Indians even when she was offered freedom.

The Obstinate Land, by Harold Keith. Crowell, 1977.
Fritz is thirteen when his family, German settlers from Texas, stake a claim in the Cherokee strip in 1893. They knew farming would be hard, but Fritz is unexpectedly thrust into adult worries when his father dies.

An Orphan for Nebraska, by Charlene J. Talbot. Atheneum, 1979.
As a homeless child in New York City in 1872, eleven-year-old Kevin is sent West on a train by the Children's Aid Society. Luckily for Kevin, he's adopted by a bachelor printer named Yule who teaches him the printing trade and shares his homestead shanty during the summer.

San Domingo: The Mexican Hat Stallion, by Marguerite Henry. Rand McNally, 1972.
Twelve-year-old Peter Lundy, growing up in the rough Nebraska Territory of the 1800s, grieves when his hostile stepfather sells his beloved horse. However, Indians take revenge on the man who bought the stallion; and Peter ends up riding the horse in the Pony Express.

Stout-Hearted Seven, by Neta L. Frazier. Harcourt, 1973.
Traveling by covered wagon to Oregon, the Sager children are determined to stay together even though their parents do not live to finish the trek.

The Thanksgiving Story, by Alice Dalgliesh. Scribner, 1954.
On the first Thanksgiving Day the Puritans celebrate their successful voyage from England to settle in the New World.

Trail through Danger, by William O. Steele. Harcourt, 1965.
Eleven-year-old Lafe Birdwell hires himself out with a hunting party to go into Cherokee territory. He wants to put to rest the rumor that his father betrayed the white men of the frontier.

Trouble River, by Betsy C. Byars. Viking, 1969.
Grandma complains about Dewey's spending so much time by the river; but when trouble comes and they have to go to a neighbor's house for help, the raft he has built is their only chance.

Winter Danger, by William O. Steele. Harcourt, 1954.

Caje's father was a woodsman born and bred, but Caje remembers living in a home with a fire and real beds.

REVOLUTIONARY WAR

Ben and Me, a New and Astonishing Life of Benjamin Franklin as Written by His Good Mouse Amos, lately discovered, edited and illustrated by Robert Lawson. Little, 1939.

Amos, close friend and constant companion of Ben Franklin, finally reveals that he, a mouse, was the one really responsible for Ben's inventions and successes.

George the Drummer Boy, by Nathaniel Benchley. Harper, 1977.

When word reaches General Gage that the Minutemen are hiding cannon and gunpowder in Concord, Massachusetts, George, a British drummer boy, goes with the soldiers in his company to capture it.

George Washington's Breakfast, by Jean Fritz. Coward, 1969.

A boy today named after George Washington is determined to find out everything he can about his namesake—including what he ate for breakfast.

I'm Deborah Sampson: A Soldier in the War of the Revolution, by Patricia Clapp. Lothrop, 1977.

Deborah Sampson disguised herself as a man, enlisted, and served for over a year as a soldier in the revolutionary army.

King George's Head Was Made of Lead, by F. N. Monjo. Coward, 1974.

From its own point of view, the statue of King George III tells about the events leading to the American Revolution.

Midnight Alarm, by Mary K. Phelan. Harper, 1968.

The two days before and the day of Paul Revere's ride to Lexington to warn John Hancock and Sam Adams that the Redcoats are coming are full of suspense and tension.

Mr. Revere and I, by Robert Lawson. Little, 1953.

The subtitle tells it all: *Being an Account of certain Episodes in the Career of PAUL REVERE, Esq. As Recently Revealed by His Horse,*

SCHEHERAZADE, Late Pride of His Royal Majesty's 14th Regiment of Foot.

Nabby Adams' Diary, by Miriam A. Bourne. Coward, 1975.

The day-to-day happenings in the John Adams's household, during the trying times when rebellion was brewing in the American colonies, are given as they might have been written by Nabby, the daughter of the house.

Rebecca's War, by Ann Finlayson. Warne, 1972.

During the British occupation of Philadelphia, fourteen-year-old Rebecca Ransome manages to outwit the British soldiers billeted in the Ransome home and keep military secrets from them.

This Time, Tempe Wick? by Patricia L. Gauch. Coward, 1974.

Tempe Wick gets mad when the mutinous revolutionary soldiers who are camped on her farm try to steal her horse, so she hides him in her bedroom.

Toliver's Secret, by Esther W. Brady. Crown, 1976.

Dressed as a boy, ten-year-old Ellen risks her life crossing the British lines with a message for General Washington concealed in a loaf of bread.

Touchmark, by Mildred Lawrence. Harcourt, 1975.

Orphaned, Nabby Jones longs to be an apprentice and make beautiful objects out of pewter; but girls must become maids, not pewterers, in 1776. However, Nabby becomes involved with the rebellion in Boston as she wheels Emily, the pewterer's crippled daughter, around the city.

Why Don't You Get a Horse, Sam Adams? by Jean Fritz. Coward, 1974.

Sam Adams was a "walker and a talker," going all over Boston trying to convince people that the colonies needed to be free and refusing to learn to ride a horse until the colonists declared their independence.

Zenas and the Shaving Mill, by F. N. Monjo. Coward, 1976.

When both British and American privateer ships (called "shaving mills") shave people clean of everything, Zenas, a Quaker boy, has to smuggle food for Nantucket Island.

WESTERNS

The Black Mustanger, by Richard Wormser. Morrow, 1971.
When Dan's father breaks his leg on the range, a quiet black man comes to his rescue. Later he teaches Dan how to catch mustangs. The secret, he says, is to be as much like a horse as possible.

Buffalo Bill, by Ingri d'Aulaire and Edgar Parin d'Aulaire. Doubleday, 1952.
Bill Cody, at twelve, is such a good rider that he gets a job with a wagon train traveling west. He meets Kit Carson, from whom he learns a great deal of trail wisdom.

Cowboys and Cattle Country, by Don Ward and J. C. Dykes. American Heritage, 1961.
The Old West and its Spanish origins are portrayed, with paintings and old photographs. There is a chapter on Wild West shows and western movies.

Granny and the Desperadoes, by Peggy Parish. Macmillan, 1970.
Pioneer Granny takes her gun and starts hunting for the thieves who took her pie. Who would think she could give them such a hard time?

How Far, Felipe? by Genevieve Gray. Harper, 1978.
In 1775, Felipe and his family travel north with Colonel Anza to what is now California, a long way to go with many hardships along the way.

Jim Bridger's Alarm Clock and Other Tall Tales, by Sid Fleischman. Dutton, 1978.
Jim, you may remember, is the man who discovered the Petrified Forest, and he insists he has seen "petrified birds . . . singing petrified songs."

Little Arliss, by Fred Gipson. Harper, 1978.
Arliss is tired of being told he is too little to do things so he defies everyone.

Mr. Mysterious and Company, by Sid Fleischman. Little, 1962.
Abracadabra Day is when the children aren't punished for anything they do.

Mr. Yowder and the Train Robbers, by Glen Rounds. Holiday, 1981.

Mr. Yowder's adventures in a ghost town out West also include one with a rattlesnake.

Old Blue, by Sibyl Hancock. Putnam, 1980.

Daniel is finally big enough to go on a trail drive with his father who is trail boss. Old Blue, a big Texas longhorn, is the lead steer for that drive and for many others.

Red Rock over the River, by Patricia Beatty. Morrow, 1973.

Dorcas and Charlie live at Fort Yuma in Arizona Territory, but Yuma City across the river always seems to have more interesting things going on; and Hattie Lou, a part Indian girl, is an interesting addition to their lives while their father is away. Secretly, Hattie Lou plans to use an ascension balloon that is part of the circus to help her half brother escape prison.

Save Queen of Sheba, by Louise Moeri. Dutton, 1981.

Traveling the Oregon Trail to catch up with Ma and Pa takes all the courage and ingenuity young King David can muster. His less than robust six-year-old sister who is with him makes the journey even more difficult.

Tree in the Trail, by Holling C. Holling. Houghton, 1942.

A lone sapling grows into a big cottonwood tree that marks the Hill-of-Peace on the Santa Fe Trail. Much of the history of the Great Plains is told through the story of this tree.

Wagon Wheels, by Barbara Brenner. Harper, 1978.

Three boys and their father travel all the way from Kentucky to Kansas. Their mother dies on the way, and the four of them have to make a home. The Kansas winter seems unusually hard to them in their dugout—and then the Indians come!

I Want Another
One like This One

THE BEST OF BEVERLY CLEARY

Beezus and Ramona, by Beverly Cleary. Morrow, 1955.

Beezus Quimby has a strong-willed four-year-old sister, Ramona, whom she admits she sometimes doesn't like. This comical story of Ramona's antics shows that you don't always have to love little sisters all the time.

Henry Huggins, by Beverly Cleary. Morrow, 1950.

Henry's bringing home a stray dog humorously changes his and his friend's lives.

Ralph S. Mouse, by Beverly Cleary. Morrow, 1982.

Ralph, a motorcycle-riding mouse, has an adventure that takes him to school where he has to prove to the class that his middle initial stands for Smart.

Ramona and Her Father, by Beverly Cleary. Morrow, 1977.

Sisters Beezus and Ramona Quimby join forces during family hard times to get Father to stop smoking.

Ramona and Her Mother, by Beverly Cleary. Morrow, 1979.

Ramona, now seven-and-a-half years old, struggles to get along with her mother, who is working full-time.

Ramona Quimby, Age 8, by Beverly Cleary. Morrow, 1981.

Being in the third grade means going to a new school, but Ramona conquers all with her stubborn spirit and a few well-chosen words.

Ramona the Pest, by Beverly Cleary. Morrow, 1968.

Ramona's individualistic reasoning constantly gets her into humorous trouble as she begins kindergarten.

FAIRY TALES LIKE
SNOW WHITE AND CINDERELLA

Beauty: A Retelling of the Story of "Beauty and the Beast," by Robin McKinley. Harper, 1978.

The appeal of this fresh, energetic retelling of the old fairy tale lies in the modern characterization of Beauty and the more mature struggle of the Beast with his "beastliness" and his "humanity."

Little Red Riding Hood, a story by the Brothers Grimm. Harcourt, 1968.

This typical, forgetful child, pudgy and homely, marches off to Grandma's; in this version both she and Grandma are rescued from the wolf.

Petrosinella, a Neapolitan Rapunzel, by Giambattista Basile, adapted by John Edward Taylor. Warne, 1981.

In this Italian version of Rapunzel three acorns are used to break the enchantment the ogress has put on the long-haired heroine.

The Princess and the Pea, by Hans Christian Andersen. Seabury, 1978.

The princess is up to the test required of her (to feel a pea under her mattress) before she can marry the prince.

The Seven Ravens, by the Brothers Grimm, with pictures by Felix Hoffman. Harcourt, 1963.

A valiant girl undertakes to remove the enchantment that has turned her brothers into ravens.

The Sleeping Beauty, retold and illustrated by Trina S. Hyman. Little, 1977.

A wicked fairy, enraged at not being invited to the Princess's christening, puts a sleeping spell on her and all the castle folk for many years. Only the right prince can break the enchantment.

The Twelve Dancing Princesses, illustrated by Adrienne Adams. Holt, 1980.

The twelve princesses outwit everyone to go dancing with their boy friends!

The Wild Swans, by Hans Christian Andersen. Dial, 1981.
A sister, by her pain and silence, releases her brothers from an enchantment.

Womenfolk and Fairy Tales, edited by Rosemary Minard.
Houghton, 1975.
These heroines take charge of their lives—from fleet Molly Whuppie, who can cross the bridge of one hair to outwit the giant, to Morgiana, the wife who engineered Ali Baba's scheme against the forty thieves.

Where Can I Find Out How to Do Things?

BALLET

Ballet Shoes, by Noel Streatfeild. Random, 1950.

The three lively little girls are not really sisters but wards of an eccentric uncle. When he disappears, Pauline, Petrova, and Posy are sent to the Children's Academy of Dancing in London to train as professional performers; but only one of them has any talent for dancing. One decides she prefers mechanics; another chooses the stage.

Frogs and the Ballet, by Donald Elliott. Gambit, 1979.

What do frogs and ballerinas have in common? Well, they both can leap gracefully! This unusual ballet book introduces the basic steps and other elements of classical ballet with a touch of humor.

I Am a Dancer, by Lynn Haney. Putnam, 1981.

Thirteen-year-old Danielle describes her life as a student at the School of American Ballet in New York. She knows that she has a great deal of hard work ahead of her but dreams of becoming a great ballerina.

If You Were a Ballet Dancer, by Ruth B. Gross. Dial, 1980.

The questions you might have about learning ballet and becoming a professional dancer are answered simply.

I'm Dancing! by Albert McCarter and Glenn Reed. Scribner, 1981.

With very simple text and photographs the book describes how scary it is to begin ballet lessons. Sometimes it hurts, but it is fun; and you can always dream of becoming a real ballerina.

Life at the Royal Ballet School, by Camilla Jessel. Metheun, 1979.

Several hundred children apply each year to attend the Royal Ballet School, but only a few are chosen. The work is very rigorous but satisfying to those who are really dedicated to dance.

My Ballet Class, by Rachel Isadora. Greenwillow, 1980.

Delicate pen-and-ink drawings describe the routine of a young girl's ballet class and introduce many ballet steps and terms.

The Nutcracker, by Warren Chappell. Knopf, 1958.

The adventure of a toy nutcracker is probably the most familiar ballet known to children. You'll be able to see the ballet live or on television, no doubt, at Christmas time, and you will appreciate the adventure of the toy nutcracker more after enjoying this book, which has illustrations and bits of music.

Samantha on Stage, by Susan C. Farrar. Dial, 1979.

Samantha, the best in her ballet class, is confident that she will get the lead in the school's production of the ballet, "The Nutcracker," until a new highly trained Russian student joins the class.

A Special Gift, by Marcia L. Simon. Harcourt, 1978.

Peter has to make a decision. Will it be basketball or will he follow his own special gift and become a ballet dancer?

A Very Young Dancer, by Jill Krementz. Knopf, 1976.

Ten-year-old Stephanie is chosen to play the leading girl in the New York City Ballet's annual production of the "The Nutcracker" ballet. An exciting look at rehearsals, costume fittings, and makeup from the other side of the curtain is given in photographs.

A Young Person's Guide to the Ballet, by Noel Streatfeild. Warne, 1975.

Two ballet students advance from learning the beginning steps to becoming senior dancers. There are also descriptions of ballet plots, films, famous people, and history.

COOKING

Betty Crocker's Cookbook for Boys and Girls. Golden Pr., 1975.

A generous number of soup to dessert recipes, both easy and advanced, are included in this standard title available in spiral-bound and paperback editions.

The Cookie Book, by Eva Moore. Houghton, 1973.

Everyone, sometime, wants to make cookies, and this cookbook suggests twelve classic cookie recipes for each of the months. All require an oven but have easy directions.

Easy Cooking: Simple Recipes for Beginning Cooks, by Ann Beebe. Morrow, 1972.

This thin book, packed with instructions and lists of necessary foods and utensils, includes recipes for fifty-one varied yet simple dishes such as candies, cookies, soups, breads, and casseroles.

How to Make Elephant Bread, by Kathy Mandry. Pantheon, 1971.

What would everyday snacks look like if they resembled the funny names given to them, for example, elephant bread (a peanut butter sandwich)?

A Jewish Cookbook for Children, by Ronnie Steinkoler. Messner, 1980.

Simple recipes and basic cooking techniques for a variety of traditional Jewish dishes especially popular during religious observances (egg kichel, matzoh balls, potato pancakes, honey cakes) have in addition explanations of the observances.

Kids Are Natural Cooks, by Parents Nursery School. Houghton, 1974.

As befits a cookbook dealing with natural foods, this one is arranged by seasons—from fall to summer—with conversational, clear directions for cooking and activities such as making butter.

Kids Cooking without a Stove, by Aileen Paul. Doubleday, 1975.

Working parents have often told their children not to use the stove, and this cookbook has many dishes, adult in nature, from chicken salad to English trifle, plus fun snacks and drinks, that are recommended for the situation.

The Kid's Diet Cookbook, by Aileen Paul. Doubleday, 1980.

An informal, conversational approach to diet, balanced meals, and calories that is evident in the many recipes ranging from breakfast to snacks.

The Kid's Kitchen Takeover, by Sara Stein. Workman, 1975.

A variety of child-tested ideas, from making fried cheese sandwiches to crystallized rose petals, can provide hours of pleasure in the kitchen.

The Little House Cookbook: Frontier Foods from Laura Ingalls
  Wilder's Classic Stories, by Barbara Walker. Harper, 1979.

The whys and hows of pioneer foods are laced with suitable quotations from the nine books in the "Little House" series. Over 100 recipes are given, much as Laura's mother made them, with changes for modern times clearly noted.

Little Witch's Black Magic Cookbook, by Linda Glovach. Prentice-
  Hall, 1972.

"Ghost Toast" or "Grape Lemonaches" are some of the snacks, and there are also five recipes for special occasions such as Mother's Day and Father's Day and, of course, Halloween.

Many Friends Cookbook: An International Cookbook for Boys and
  Girls, by Terry Cooper and Marilyn Ratner. Philomel, in cooperation with the U.S. Committee for UNICEF, 1980.

One to three spoons denote the level of difficulty for making soup, sandwiches, and entrees from thirty-two countries and six regions of the United States; but most of the recipes are not for novices.

The Pooh Cook Book, by Virginia H. Ellison. Dell, 1975.

This collection, inspried by Winnie-the-Pooh, the character created by A. A. Milne, features over sixty recipes with appropriate quotations.

The Storybook Cookbook, by Carol MacGregor. Doubleday, 1967.

There are twenty-two recipes in this cookbook for food that popular book characters have eaten, such as Uncle Ulysses' doughnuts and Dorothy's scrambled eggs.

DRAWING

Cartooning for Kids, by Carol Lea Benjamin. Crowell, 1982.

A cartoonist shows how to make funny, simple drawings of animals and people.

Cats and How to Draw Them, by Amy Hogeboom. Vanguard, 1949.

Cats are described by breed with a photographic pose. Then, in a series of steps using ovals and lines, the author explains how to draw the figures.

Drawing Dogs and Puppies, by Paul Frame. Watts, 1978.

The author suggests looking observantly at your surroundings, practicing drawing often, and learning something of different breeds and positions of dogs.

Drawing with Numbers and Letters, by Rebecca Emberley. Little, 1981.

An unusual, clearly illustrated drawing book shows how to put numbers and letters together to make charming animals.

Ed Emberley's Drawing Book of Faces, by Ed Emberley. Little, 1975.

Using basic shapes, Emberley shows a step-by-step method of drawing faces. Cartooning ideas are given, plus dozens of faces.

Going for a Walk with a Line, by Douglas MacAgy and Elizabeth MacAgy. Doubleday, 1959.

An artist uses a "line" to make many kinds of pictures to tell stories or ideas or to show feelings. A group of very interesting modern art masterpieces is used to show different art styles.

How to Draw Dogs, Cats and Horses, by Arthur Zaidenberg. Harper, 1959.

Zaidenberg believes anyone who understands animals can draw them. He describes the basic drawing materials, demonstrates how to construct the forms and place them in proper relation to each other, and instructs the drawer to put into this general shape what he or she "sees" as the essence of the animal.

The I-Can't-Draw-Book, by Jerry Warshaw. Albert Whitman, 1971.

By using certain items for tracing, such as a hammer, a padlock, or even your own hand, Warshaw introduces more creative forms and objects. A triangle and a circle become a cat or a person; squiggles turn into unusual fish.

Make 25 Crayon Drawings of the Circus, by Lee J. Ames. Doubleday, 1980.

You will like drawing the bright circus cartoons with crayons that make warm, fuzzy drawings.

Pastels Are Great! by John Hawkinson. Albert Whitman, 1968.

Many color illustrations showing pastels as an artistic medium delight the eye. Warm-ups are followed by instructions in the eight basic strokes and directions for combining strokes to form real and imaginary animals and other designs.

HOW TO MAKE THINGS

Easy Embroidery, by Lis Paludan. Taplinger, 1970.

In addition to the basics of embroidery there are sections on making patterns, using other materials such as felt and cord, painting on cloth, and finishing off edges. There are twenty-five pages of patterns and a list of stitches.

Jewish Holiday Crafts, by Joyce Becker. Hebrew Pub., 1977.

There are over 200 ideas in this book and precise instructions for crafts whose materials will be available around the house. The text also describes the various Jewish holidays.

The Little Witch's Birthday Book, by Linda Glovach. Prentice-Hall, 1981.

Do you know how to have a surprise birthday-in-bed party for a friend who is sick? Do you want to have a real "little witch" party for yourself or a friend? The Goblin will show you how to make costumes and birthday treats.

Making Musical Things, by Ann Wiseman. Scribner, 1979.

Make drums from pots, xylophones from wood, guitars from milk cartons, and other melodious creations.

Making Things Book 2, Handbook of Creative Discovery, by Ann Wiseman. Little, 1975.

Among the activities described and illustrated are sewing, bookmaking, furniture building, cooking, and beadwork; and among the materials used are clay, soap, and tin cans.

Messing Around with Drinking Straw Construction, by Bernie Zubrowski. Little, 1981.

What keeps a skyscraper from falling down or a bridge from falling over? What's the most stable shape for a roof? This is an activity book to show how to build your own models out of drinking straws.

Piñatas, by Virginia Brock. Abingdon, 1966.

Filled with candy or surprise gifts, piñatas are pretty and mysterious and made to be broken. Did you know that one Spanish explorer was saved from death at the hands of hostile Indians because he gave them a piñata from his native country? History, stories, and directions for making piñatas are in this book.

HOW TO SAY THINGS

A Book of Kisses, by Dave Ross. Random, 1982.

A laughable look at kissing—its history, how to kiss, when to kiss, kinds of kisses, and what to do to stop being kissed (wear a necklace made of garlic).

Dandelions Don't Bite, by Leone Adelson. Pantheon, 1972.

The introduction discusses language, words, and communication in general; and it is followed with brief discussions of the origins, spelling, and meanings of words.

Handtalk: An ABC of Finger Spelling and Sign Language, by Remy Charlip and others. Scholastic, 1974.

Close-up photos of hands make this a clear and useful presentation of the basic finger spelling and sign language used by deaf people.

Hieroglyphs for Fun, Your Own Secret Code Language, by Joseph Scott and Lenore Scott. Van Nostrand, 1974.

The basic twenty-four-letter hieroglyphic alphabet and the English sounds represented are included with a brief discussion of various aspects of Egyptian culture.

High on a Hill, selected by Ed Young. Philomel, 1980.

Authentic Chinese riddles combine humor with learning about another culture and language.

How Ships Play Cards, a Beginning Book of Homonyms, by Cynthia Basil. Morrow, 1980.

Riddles introduce words that look and sound alike but have different meanings.

How to Keep a Secret, by Elizabeth James and Carol Barkin. Lothrop, 1978.

Secret spoken language, alphabets, coding devices, signals, and hiding places are highlighted. Many kinds of invisible writing are explained as well as transposition and alphabet-substitution ciphers. A final chapter decodes secret messages found throughout the text.

How to Make Your Own Books, by Harvey Weiss. Crowell, 1974.

The author tells how to select and assemble paper for the pages and how to make covers and put it all together as well as suggesting appropriate subjects for your very own book.

In Other Words: A Junior Thesaurus, by W. Cabell Greet and others. Scott, Foresman, 1969.
Some 100 common words and 1000 synonyms and antonyms help expand your vocabulary.

Indian Picture Writings, by Robert Hofsinde (Gray-Wolf). Morrow, 1959.
Samples from 248 basic American Indian picture-symbols, which contain information about the culture, encourage the reader to try to learn this language.

Jambo Means Hello, by Muriel Feelings. Dial, 1974.
After a brief introduction on where Swahili is spoken in Africa, there is one word for each of the twenty-four letters in the Swahili alphabet. Each letter is also accompanied by an illustrated definition.

Put Your Foot in Your Mouth, and Other Silly Sayings, by James A. Cox. Random, 1980.
The origin and meaning of twenty-one idioms used in American English such as "blow your own horn" and "too big for your britches" are discussed.

The Signed English Dictionary for Preschool and Elementary Levels, edited by Harry Bornstein and others. Gallaudet College Pr., 1975.
A very complete reference book with nearly 300 pages of signed English that have approximately eight illustrations and brief directions on each page, the book also has additional references and explanations about signed English.

There Is a Bull on My Balcony (Hay un Toro en Mi Balcón), by Sesyle Joslin. Harcourt, 1966.
This is a humorous introduction to Spain and its language.

What? A Riddle Book, by Jane Sarnoff. Scribner, 1974.
Unusual illustrations make this book almost as much fun to look at as it is to read. An example of the riddles is: "Where do old Volkswagens go? To the old Volks' home."

MAGIC

Big Anthony and the Magic Ring, by Tomie de Paola. Harcourt, 1979.

Big Anthony and Strega Nona, the witch, are at it again. Using a stolen magic ring, he becomes Handsome Big Anthony—experiencing night life and adoring ladies wanting to dance with him. Only Strega Nona can help him out of this scrape.

Black and Blue Magic, by Zilpha K. Snyder. Atheneum, 1972.

Harry Houdini Marco (named after the magician) drinks a magic liquid that makes him sprout wings and fly. At first the situation looks perfect, but not everything turns out as expected.

Break a Magic Circle, by Elizabeth Johnson. Little, 1971.

Tilly and David believe in Robert although he is invisible when he seeks their help. Restoring the broken mushroom circle will counteract the fury of the strange little man who made him invisible. Otherwise, he will be invisible for twenty years.

Dorrie and the Amazing Magic Elixir, by Patricia Coombs. Lothrop, 1974.

Dorrie manages to prevent the Green Wizard from stealing the "hex-proof, spell-proof, potion-proof" Magic Elixir but not before he turns her and her helper into toads while Dorrie's mother, Big Witch, is out gathering moon herbs.

The First Book of Magic, by Edward Stoddard. Watts, 1977.

You can perform all the magic tricks in this book with simple, inexpensive objects readily found at home. Directions thoroughly explain and illustrate the tricks with step-by-step sketches and diagrams and an emphasis on rules to avoid misdirection.

Give a Magic Show! by Burton Marks and Rita Marks. Lothrop, 1977.

This book contains all the information you need to put on a successful magic show, including staging and instructions for making a costume, hat, and wand. Directions tell how to do seventeen tricks and how to prepare for each trick before the show.

The Great Custard Pie Panic, by Scott Corbett. Little, 1974.

The last time the fog was up, it had meant trouble for Nick and his dog. This time the fog carries the irresistible smell of freshly baked bread. Curious, Nick and Bert soon meet an old enemy with a score to settle.

Magic Camera, by Daniel M. Pinkwater. Dodd, 1974.
Charles's father gives him an old camera from the cellar to play with while he's sick. It has knobs, cranks, buttons, and switches and looks magical to him. That night a click of the switch leads Charles into a magical adventure.

The Magic Mirrors, by Judith B. Griffin. Coward, 1971.
Beloved Princess Aminatou receives two magic mirrors on her twelfth birthday—one from the moon showing the past, the other from the sun revealing the future. When her jealous stepmother plots revenge using evil magic, Aminatou risks great danger to free her brother, sixty warriors, and their horses from the medicine man's spell.

Magic . . . Naturally: Science Entertainments and Amusements, by Vicki Cobb. Harper, 1976.
Learn about physics, chemistry, and psychology in doing thirty entertaining magic tricks for which clear concise directions are given.

Seven-Day Magic, by Edward Eager. Harcourt, 1962.
An ordinary book checked out of the library turns out to be magical. When a group of children open it and read, it turns out to be about them. They learn how to use it and go back in time to a one-room schoolhouse and forward to watch their father's TV show in New York.

Spooky Tricks, by Rose Wyler and Gerald Ames. Harper, 1968.
How to make a girl disappear from a box, a boy float in the air, a ghost appear on the wall, and cats sparkle in the dark are some of the spooky tricks you can learn, all of which are clearly explained.

What the Witch Left, by Ruth Chew. Scholastic, 1974.
Kathy and Louise unlock an old chest drawer that they are told not to disturb. Inside there are ordinary objects such as gloves, a bathrobe, and a tin box. These ordinary-looking objects get the girls into a series of magical adventures and even a visit from a witch.

PUPPETS

*Making Puppets Come Alive: A Method of Learning and Teaching
Hand Puppetry,* by Larry Engler and Carol Fijan. Taplinger,
1973.
Convincing photographs demonstrate the step-by-step instructions for making puppets move.

The Master Puppeteer, by Katherine Paterson. Harper, 1975.
A young Japanese boy gets an inside look at the workings of a professional pupper theater while a civil war is being waged around him.

Pinocchio, by Carlo Collodi. Four Winds, 1981.
A mischevious marionette becomes a real boy after a near-death episode with robbers but only after he also stops lying (which caused his nose to grow) and helps his father regain his health.

The Rooster's Horns: A Chinese Puppet Play to Make and Perform, by
Ed Young and Hillary Becket. Philomel, 1978.
A Chinese folktale about a rooster, a dragon, and a worm is followed by instructions for making and performing a shadow puppet play of the story.

Scrap Puppets: How to Make and Move Them, by Laura Ross. Holt,
1978.
Start with the contents of a box of scraps and learn to make and operate hand, rod, and shadow puppets and marionettes.

Song, Speech and Ventriloquism, by Larry Kettelkamp. Morrow,
1967.
In addition to telling how your voice works while talking and while singing, this book also gives an introduction to how to use your voice like a ventriloquist.

Where Are the Cycle Books?

The Bicycle Man, by Allen Say. Houghton, 1982.

Children at a Japanese school meet two American soldiers just after World War II during a sportsday in which one soldier participates for the pleasure of showing his riding expertise.

Dirt Bikes, by Ray Hill. Golden Pr., 1974.

Logically, most bikes are made for either paved roads or rough terrain; and various types of off-road riding require specific bikes, many of which are shown in this book with color photographs, specifications, and comments.

Drag Racing for Beginners, by I. G. Edmonds. Bobbs-Merrill, 1972.

For competition, drivers alter their engines to increase the speeds of their cars; but the types of wheels, bodies, fuels, and drivers also figure in achieving speeds of nearly 300 miles per hour.

A Great Bicycle Book, by Jane Sarnoff and Reynold Ruffins. Scribner, 1976.

The whole and the parts of a bicycle need your care and understanding if you want to enjoy it and perhaps race it.

Motorcycle Racing, by Nicole Puleo. Lerner, 1973.

About ten types of race competitions for motorcycles are explained with approximately half of them given a one-page description plus a color photograph. Endurance, dirt track, cross-country, and scramble racing have longer descriptions.

Some Basics about Motorcycles, by Ed Radlauer. Childrens Pr., 1978.

Although not alphabetical in arrangement, this book is almost a dictionary of terms about motorcycles, written in a friendly style with lots of information and small color photographs.

Trailbiking, by Peter B. Mohn. Crestwood, 1975.

You can enjoy off-road motorcycling (trailbiking) if you are not old enough to ride a minibike on the streets. Bikes differ according to purposes—more power needed for hills, for example, versus traffic use. Competing is also covered.

I Want a
Short Book

Frog and Toad Are Friends, by Arnold Lobel. Harper, 1970.
Friends Frog and Toad have five adventures in this book, and in one of these they help each other when they are sick.

The Gang and Mrs. Higgins, by George Shannon. Greenwillow, 1981.
Mrs. Higgins hides a bag of gold in a place where the robber gang never dreams of looking.

The Gollywhopper Egg, by Anne Rockwell. Macmillan, 1974.
Farmer Foote tries all kinds of ways to hatch a coconut he bought from peddler Timothy Toad into a gollywhopper.

Help! You're Shrinking, by Edward Packard. Bantam, 1983.
Whoever heard of an author telling you to skip some pages in his book? He gives you choices of which pages to read and which to skip according to the way you want the story to go.

Leo, Zack, and Emmie, by Amy Ehrlich. Dial, 1981.
The new girl in class, Emmie Williams, can wiggle her ears and say the names of all the dinosaurs. Leo and Zack think she's great, but when they find that only two can be partners at once, Zack is the one left out.

Play Ball, Amelia Bedelia, by Peggy Parish. Harper, 1972.
Amelia Bedelia, the absentminded housekeeper, substitutes for a

sick player on the Grizzlies baseball team. Her efforts to tag a runner, put a man out, and run home cause chaos.

Quimble Wood, by N. M. Bodecker. Atheneum, 1981.
   Quimbles are wee folk who wear tall, pointed hats and stand "no bigger than your little finger." Four of them, Quilliam, Quilice, Quint, and Quenelope, must set up a forest home after they have been left accidentally behind at the roadside.

Tales of Oliver Pig, by Jean Van Leeuwen. Dial, 1979.
   Oliver Pig and his sister Amanda have good days (baking cookies or grandmother's visit). A bad day is when Oliver *almost* forgets to share with Amanda *all* day.

Troll Country, by Edward Marshall. Dial, 1980.
   Elsie Fay's book tells all about trolls, and her mother tells her she met one once. When Elsie Fay goes by the woods, she looks for a troll and finds one.

Worthington Botts and the Steam Machine, by Betty Baker. Macmillan, 1981.
   Worthington Botts reads all the time, even while he is playing baseball and doing chores. He builds a steam machine to do his tasks; but it frightens the cow, pulls up the roses, and runs after the baseball players.

SKINNY

Chasing after Annie, by Marjorie W. Sharmat. Harper, 1981.
   Bigheaded but likeable Richie is convinced that cute little Annie is crazy about him and writes it in his journal. Annie's diary, on the other hand, indicates that she absolutely cannot stand him. When Annie's dog disappears, Richie, playing hero, really messes up.

A Game of Catch, by Helen Cresswell. Macmillan, 1977.
   Kate and Hugh are walking through an empty museum when they hear some mysterious laughter. Could it be the children who are playing ball in an eighteenth-century painting? When they return to the picture, Kate is astounded to see the ball in it is in a different position.

Graham Oakley's Magical Changes, by Graham Oakley. Atheneum, 1980.

Absolutely without words, this is a mix and match, a strange and gorgeous book, but not for the very young, the faint of heart, or the humorless.

The Hoboken Chicken Emergency, by Daniel M. Pinkwater. Prentice-Hall, 1977.

What do you do with a 266-pound (and still growing) chicken, supposed to be a Thanksgiving turkey, who runs amok? Only Pinkwater could come up with a clucking King Kong and give you a happy (could you believe logical?) ending.

I Will Make You Disappear, by Carol B. York. Nelson, 1974.

"By the seven powers of the seven powers of darkness, I will make you disappear. Mandrake root and pure earth; I will make you disappear." The power of the chant engulfs three children and their mother in a summer house haunted by witchcraft, hidden treasure, and a menacing handyman.

Mary of Mile 18, by Ann Blades. Tundra, 1971.

Because life is so hard in their village in northern Canada, Mary's father refuses to let her keep the puppy she finds until it has proven its usefulness.

McBroom Tells a Lie, by Sid Fleischman. Little, 1976.

The lie has nothing to do with saving his wonderful one-acre farm from Heck Jones, his neighbor who covets it so much that he steals some of the topsoil in a cane and on his shoes, but McBroom admits he has told one.

Peter Penny's Dance, by Janet Quin-Harkin. Dial, 1976.

Dancing the hornpipe was better than a sailor's work so Peter Penny bet the captain he could dance around the world; and if he could in five years, he could marry Lavinia, the captain's daughter.

Petronella, by Jay Williams. Parents, 1973.

We all know how fairy tales work: the king's third son rides off to rescue a princess and marry her and they live happily ever after. But what if the third son is a daughter? And what if the handsome prince is a twit?

The Phantom Ice Cream Man, by X. J. Kennedy. Atheneum, 1979.

There are a lot of great skinny poetry books (and some terrific fat ones, too); this is one nonsensical one.

The Reluctant Dragon, by Kenneth Grahame. Holiday, 1953.

Take one dragon who prefers not to fight; a passel of frightened villagers; a boy who does not judge by appearances; the established hero, St. George, hired to wipe out said dragon; and you have what may be the best dragon story ever written unless, of course, you insist on fierce dragons.

Time-Ago Lost: More Tales of Jahdu, by Virginia Hamilton. Macmillan, 1973.

Mama Luka tells her stories of time-ago, and one is the story of how clever little Jahdu deals with the giant Trouble.

Where Was Patrick Henry on the 29th of May? by Jean Fritz. Coward, 1975.

Throughout his life Patrick Henry remembered the exciting day that he became a firebrand of the Revolution instead of a tongue-tied young lawyer.

Wiley and the Hairy Man, adapted from an American folktale by Molly G. Bang. Macmillan 1976.

The Hairy Man is a monster that lives in the swamp where Wiley cuts bamboo poles, and his hound dogs save him from it twice. The next time, however, the monster comes to the house, and Wiley's mother has to deal with it.

I Want a Mystery

MYSTERIES

Be a Super Sleuth with the Face at the Window, by Wolfgang Ecke. Metheun, 1978.

The fifteen short mystery stories have all the clues you need to solve them; don't worry, the answers are in the back of the book, and each mystery is graded according to its difficulty.

Benny Uncovers a Mystery, by Gertrude C. Warner. Albert Whitman, 1976.

When Benny and Henry get summer jobs at the local department store, they soon find themselves plunged into some strange happenings.

The Case of the Elevator Duck, by Polly B. Berends. Random, 1973.

Gilbert, a young amateur detective, finds a duck in his housing project elevator. His mother gives him three days to find the owner, but who is willing to admit ownership in a building where pets are not allowed?

The Case of the Secret Scribbler, by E. W. Hildick. Macmillan, 1978.

McGurk and friends solve a robbery before it happens, with good thinking and some scientific detecting by Brains, the newest member of their organization.

The Day the Sea Rolled Back, by Mickey Spillane. Windmill, 1979.

When an unexplainable event causes the ocean water to recede around Peolle Island in the Caribbean, Larry and his friend Josh set off to explore the incredible terrain of the ocean floor, pursued by villainous treasure hunters.

Einstein Anderson Makes Up for Lost Time, by Seymour Simon. Viking, 1981.

The ten puzzles solved scientifically by Adam "Einstein" Anderson include a way to use a watch as a compass when lost and the exposé of a professor with a machine that supposedly stops hurricanes.

Encyclopedia Brown: Boy Detective, by Donald J. Sobol. Elsevier-Nelson, 1963.

A fifth-grader, who is the son of the chief of police and a complete library walking around in sneakers, naturally sets himself up in the detective business in Laville in the summer. There are nine cases with solutions for each in the back of the book.

Express Train to Trouble, by Robert Quackenbush. Prentice-Hall, 1981.

When Ruddy Duck disappears on an express train to Cairo, Miss Mallard uses her detective genius to solve the mystery à la Christie.

From the Mixed-up Files of Mrs. Basil E. Frankweiler, by E. L. Konigsburg. Atheneum, 1967.

When Claudia runs away from home with her brother Jamie and they hide in the Metropolitan Museum of Art, part of the adventure is an attempt to discover the sculptor of a beautiful little angel.

The Ghost on Saturday Night, by Sid Fleischman. Little, 1974.

The townspeople of Golden Hill, California, famous for its thick fogs, are anticipating a traveling show displaying the ghost of Crookneck John. Opie, one of the town's best "fog" guides, begins to suspect that the show is also the cover for a bank robbery and is able to use his special skills to foil the plans.

Howliday Inn, by James Howe. Atheneum, 1982.

The mysterious disappearance of various canine guests at the Chateau Bow-Wow, where they are staying for a week, has Harold and Chester doing some hilarious detecting.

The Mysterious Disappearance of Leon: (I Mean Noel), by Ellen Raskin. Dutton, 1971.

The young Mrs. Carillon searches for her husband, following a bizarre collection of clues, and collects twin children, a taste for

Chinese restaurants, and vast travel knowledge along the way. Asterisked notes point out pertinent clues throughout the book.

A Summer in the South, by James Marshall. Houghton, 1977.

A small hotel on a quiet beach holds an assortment of guests who are not all that they seem. Eleanor Owl, a famed detective, and her assistant, Mr. Paws, surreptitiously question the guests about some puzzling events connected with the Egyptian treasure of the Great Kluk.

SPIES

Adventures in Black, by Arthur Widder. Harper, 1962.

The nearly incredible stories of famous real spies throughout the years, especially during World War II, make fascinating reading. Told in great detail, the cruelties and torture rather than the glamour are stressed.

The Alligator Case, by William Pène du Bois. Harper, 1965.

A young detective's first case is about alligators—lots and lots of alligators, including possibly thieves who may have used alligator costumes.

Alvin's Secret Code, by Clifford B. Hicks. Holt, 1963.

Twelve-year-old Alvin and his best friend Shoie become adept at codes and ciphers under the tutelage of Mr. Link, an Allied spy in World War II. When news of a treasure, stolen during the Civil War, becomes known, the two friends apply their deductive powers to finding it. There are a number of code and cipher exercises at the back of the book.

Dead before Docking, by Scott Corbett. Little, 1972.

Lip-reading, Jeff "overhears" part of a telephone conversation convincing him that someone aboard the ship with him will be "dead before docking."

Harriet the Spy, by Louise Fitzhugh. Harper, 1964.

Harriet takes copious notes about everyone she "spies" on but does not get into trouble until she becomes editor of the Sixth Grade Page of her school paper.

Libby Shadows a Lady, by Catherine Woolley. Morrow, 1974.

After overhearing a bomb threat, Libby spends her Easter vacation tracking a woman and manages to foil a kidnapping while trying to find out what the woman meant when she said over the phone she was going to bomb the Federal Reserve Bank.

Phoebe and the General, by Judith Griffin. Coward, 1977.

Phoebe, whose father is an innkeeper, is told to watch for a man whose name begins with T and foils a plot on General Washington's life.

The Remarkable Return of Winston Potter Crisply, by Eve Rice. Greenwillow, 1978.

Wondering what their brother is up to, Max and Becky follow him all over New York. Is he a spy? Are the Russians after him?

Toliver's Secret, by Esther W. Brady. Crown, 1976.

During the Revolutionary War ten-year-old Ellie is given the dangerous task of smuggling a message through Redcoat lines while disguised as a boy.

War Work, by Libby Oneal. Viking, 1971.

Zoe, her little sister Rosie, and their friend Joe decide to contribute to the World War II effort by tracking enemy spies in their small Midwestern town.

I Want a Sad Story

Autumn Street, by Lois Lowry. Houghton, 1980.

When Elizabeth is six, the answer to anything upsetting is "it's the war." Her family moves to her grandparents' house, and her daddy leaves for the Pacific front; but she finds her greatest sorrow, her friend Charles' death, is not caused by the war.

The 18th Emergency, by Betsy C. Byars. Viking, 1973.

Mouse, our hero, living in terror of being beaten by the school bully, Hammerman, dreams up incredibly impossible solutions to his dilemma.

Fanny's Sister, by Penelope Lively. Dutton, 1980.

Eight-year-old Fanny is the oldest of six Victorian children. When another baby comes, in her prayers for cherry tart she lets God know that she would not mind if He took the baby back. When dessert *is* cherry tart, she must face her guilty fears.

The Gift-Giver, by Joyce Hansen. Houghton, 1980.

Amir, a foster child, with patience and perception changes the lives of the children on 163rd Street at the end of fifth grade and the beginning of sixth grade before he moves on again.

Grandmama's Joy, by Eloise Greenfield. Philomel, 1980.

Rhondy and Grandmama have only each other; but when hard times come and they must move, each other is all they need.

Growing Anyway Up, by Florence P. Heide. Harper, 1976.

Florence has rituals to make places, people, and situations "safe"— nonthreatening. Since her father's death, she and her mother have lived alone until they move from Florida to Pennsylvania where her mother meets and eventually marries George. Florence meets Aunt Nina, and that makes all the difference.

The Jazz Man, by Mary H. Weik. Atheneum, 1966.

Zeke, aged nine, lives on the top floor of a Harlem brownstone and seldom goes out becuase of his lame leg; his days are made richer by his new neighbor's piano music. Everyone deserts him one night, but he awakes to his parents' return and to music.

Julia and the Third Bad Thing, by Barbara B. Wallace. Follett, 1975.

Julia is afraid after her grandmother says bad things come in threes. When her sister Anicia is burned, Katya's first piano lesson is cancelled without explanation, and her mother becomes ill, her dread mounts to real fear.

The Life (and Death) of Sarah Elizabeth Harwood, by Mary Q. Steele. Greenwillow, 1980.

Sarah's problems seem insurmountable. Not only has she lost a friend's flower album, but she also is overwhelmed by the realization of people's mortality brought on by her brother's near-miss with death. Maybe it would be easier just to die now!

P.S. Write Soon, by Colby Rodowsky. Watts, 1978.

Tanner Mary McClean's letters to the fifth-grade pen pal she has never met tell of how she wishes her life to be rather than how it is. Youngest in a big, busy family, she has only a few friends, a new, shy sister-in-law, and a brace on her leg that prohibits sports.

The Saving of P.S., by Robbie Branscum. Doubleday, 1977.

As P.S. (Priscilla Sue) tells it, she's a misfit in her family! This twelve-year-old Arkansas girl keeps house for her widowed preacher father until he remarries, and then she feels even more out of place.

The Velveteen Rabbit, by Margery Williams. Doubleday, 1958.

A toy rabbit, much loved by its owner, the Boy, becomes real. He meets real rabbits and sees the Boy again but cannot avoid his own death.

I Want an
Exciting Story

ABOUT THE FUTURE

A Book of Flying Saucers for You, by Franklyn M. Branley. Crowell,
  1973.
  Sightings of UFOs and the reasons behind such phenomena, life
in outer space, and the difficulties of and the possible solutions to
long distance travel are examined.

The Deadly Hoax, by Scott Corbett. Dutton, 1981.
  Morgan and his friend Sid are alone when mysterious messages
begin to come in on their home computer screen. Five strange intrud-
ers state their mission: "We will persuade Earthlings to accept the
temporary domination of superior powers. . . . "

Exiled from Earth, by Ben Bova. Dutton, 1971.
  Courageous but desperate scientists, generations from now, have
their dream of distant colonization come true. The books in this
series, inextricably woven together, must be regarded as one unit,
especially for the powerful last volume to have its full impact.

Fat Men from Space, by Daniel M. Pinkwater. Dodd, 1977.
  The new filling in William's tooth acts like a tiny built-in radio.
This is a problem for him in school when he can't shut if off. It picks
up signals from men from the planet Spiegel, who love junk food
from Earth.

Investigating UFO's, by Larry Kettelkamp. Morrow, 1971.
  This presentation of UFOs is directed toward a description of the

many individual sightings of flying saucers, the kinds that have been reported, and the Air Force investigations. The accounts of human contact with humanoids are particularly fascinating.

My Robot Buddy, by Alfred Slote. Lippincott, 1975.
For his tenth birthday Jack gets his very own robot that looks just like a real boy and is programmed for fourth grade. Danny One can play baseball and basketball, climb trees and fish, converse, and do light household chores.

Next Stop Earth, by William E. Butterworth. Walker, 1978.
Charley and his little sister Julie are in a space ship hurtling toward earth. They can't find their father, the pilot; and when Charley questions the computer, it replies, "Malfunction. Does not Compute."

The Third Planet from Altair, by Edward Packard. Harper, 1979.
Who is sending messages from outer space? You can choose your own adventures in this story about a spaceship and its crew in search of the source of the mysterious messages.

UFOs: A Pictorial History from Antiquity to the Present, by David C. Knight. McGraw-Hill, 1979.
Read the captions and look at the fascinating pictures from start to finish in order to learn about the whole sweep of UFO history, including the fakes, in this well-researched, well-documented account.

The White Mountains, by John Christopher. Macmillan, 1967.
In a village of the future one is not supposed to think for oneself. At the age of fourteen everyone must have a steel cap implanted in his or her skull through which the hated monster Tripods can control all thoughts. Three boys try to escape.

ESP

And This Is Laura, by Ellen Conford. Little, 1977.
Fearing that she does not have any talents in a family of achievers, Laura is overjoyed to find that she has psychic powers. Success and popularity follow; but then the powers turn against her, and she must find a solution to her dilemma.

Beloved Benjamin Is Waiting, by Jean E. Karl. Dutton, 1978.

Deserted by her parents and fearful, Lucinda finds refuge in an abandoned building in a nearby cemetery where she makes contact with outer-space life through the broken statue of a young boy who died many years ago.

Evy-Ivy-Over, by Colby Rodowsky. Watts, 1978.

Torn by a desire for acceptance by her peers and loyalty to her beloved grandmother who is rearing her, Slug faces the fact that being able to see things others cannot need not isolate her from them.

The Forever Formula, by Frank Bonham. Dutton, 1979.

Two centuries earlier Evan was put in suspended animation; now, he awakens to a world in which the secret of everlasting youth is passionately sought. The formula for this, developed by Evan's late father, is locked in his mind; and evil rulers are determined to destroy him to obtain it.

The Forgotten Door, by Alexander Key. Westminster, 1965.

When a boy falls to earth from another planet, the people he meets here are so suspicious of his ability to talk to animals, to read minds, and to run at superspeed that they become hostile. His rescuers are an understanding family who must make an important choice.

The Ghosts of Austwick Manor, by Reby E. MacDonald. Atheneum, 1982.

Hillary and Heather are the first of the MacDonalds to step back in time by way of a scale model of the MacDonald castle; later they persuade their older brother Donald, who is the heir, to go with them, not once but twice, in order to remove the fatal curse on their generation.

The Gift, by Peter Dickinson. Little, 1973.

Clairvoyance is inherited in Davy Price's family, and he is a bearer. His very ordinary, unsuccessful father is tempted to crime and pursued by a mad killer; and Davy knows it all because he can "see" into the minds of others.

A Gift of Magic, by Lois Duncan. Little, 1971.

On her deathbed Nancy's grandmother gives her the gift of ESP. She tries unsuccessfully to hide her talent from adults and particularly from her teacher, who is courting her divorced mother; but in the end she must use it to save her younger brother's life.

The Girl with the Silver Eyes, by Willo D. Roberts. Atheneum, 1980.

The satisfaction that unhappy Katie gains by moving objects through thought, thereby terrorizing and frustrating the adults who do not please her, is only secondary to her realization that there are other children like her. She must find them.

The Hocus-Pocus Dilemma, by Pat Kibbe. Knopf, 1979.

When ten-year-old B. J. suddenly discovers she has ESP, she embraces her new powers wholeheartedly. A crystal ball, a horoscope, and books on fortune-telling embark her on a career that touches her entire family, including Willie the dog, with often dire but hilarious consequences.

Into the Dream, by William Sleator. Dutton, 1979.

In an often terrifying series of events, two children dream the same dream, find they can read each others' minds, and eventually rescue from exploiters a small child who was also exposed to a previous brief UFO visit that even affected a pet dog.

The Perilous Gard, by Elizabeth M. Pope. Houghton, 1974.

Kate is a sensible girl who finds her intelligence is very important in overcoming superstitions surrounding All Hallows' Eve and the Holy Well of Elvenwood Hall to which she has been banished by Queen Mary of England.

Sixth Sense, by Larry Kettelkamp. Morrow, 1970.

Well-known events that were predicted by ESP, such as the Titanic disaster, and the famous people who have been involved in the investigation of psychic powers are especially interesting.

SCIENCE FICTION

C.O.L.A.R., by Alfred Slote. Lippincott, 1981.

Jack and Danny stumble on to a colony of runaway robot children and work to find a way to let them keep their freedom.

The Delikon, by H. M. Hoover. Viking, 1977.

The Delikon society from outer space has ruled earth for centuries, sending their teachers here to train children for leadership. Caught up in a revolution against the Delikon, two children and Varnia, their teacher, make a perilous escape.

The Donkey Planet, by Scott Corbett. Dutton, 1979.

Two young scientists, one disguised as a boy with horns and the other as a donkey, travel to a distant planet to get some "quundar" and end up getting in trouble.

Dragonfall 5 and the Empty Planet, by Brian Earnshaw. Lothrop, 1976.

Tim and Sanchez, grounded for four weeks to attend school, manage to stir things up on the boringest planet in the universe when some of their classmates disappear.

The Fallen Spaceman, by Lee Harding. Harper, 1980.

Deep inside a giant spacesuit is a tiny alien who accidentally falls to earth from a passing spaceship. Alone and frightened, unable to leave the special atmosphere of the suit, he is befriended by a boy who travels with him during his short stay here.

Is There Life on a Plastic Planet? by Mildred Ames. Dutton, 1975.

What first appeared to be a blissful escape from their parents for Hollis and her cousin turns into horror when the robots who replace them in the activities they do not like take over their entire lives and relegate them to a meaningless existence.

Matthew Looney's Voyage to the Earth, by Jerome Beatty, Jr. Avon, 1972.

Matt, a moon child, gets into trouble when he sneaks his pet murtle aboard the first Earth Expeditionary Force and loses him in the strange tides on earth.

Miss Pickerell Goes to Mars, by Ellen MacGregor. McGraw, 1951.

Timid, grandmotherly, and old-fashioned, Miss Pickerell investigates a huge rocketship standing in the field on her farm. Once hidden inside, she finds herself taking off for Mars with the spaceship crew.

My Trip to Alpha I, by Alfred Slote. Lippincott, 1978.

Traveling by VOYA-CODE enables a person to send his or her "mind" by computer to a substitute body at the other end of the journey. Jack travels to another planet to visit his aunt, using this new form of space travel, and runs into danger and a mystery he must solve.

Star Ka'at World, by Andre Norton and Dorothy Madlee. Walker, 1976.

Jim Evans and Elly Mae visit the planet of the Ka'ats and by helping them destroy the Hsi City of Death become true Ka'atkin.

TIME CHANGES

A Chance Child, by Jill P. Walsh. Farrar, 1978.
Creep escapes from cruel treatment at home to an adventure with children from a century earlier when many children worked all day in the mines and factories for their daily bread.

The Children of Green Knowe, by L. M. Boston. Harcourt, 1967.
When Tolly comes to visit his great-grandmother in her very old house, he discovers he is not the only child living at Green Knowe. Toby, Linnet, and Alexander, who played there in the seventeenth century, may never have left!

The Court of the Stone Children, by Eleanor Cameron. Dutton, 1973.
Nina loves to wander about in a museum in San Francisco, playing imaginary games. She sees a strange, beautiful girl whom she learns lived in a French chateau more than a century earlier.

Fog Magic, by Julia L. Sauer. Archway, 1977.
Greta has always loved the fog, and one very foggy day she goes over the mountain into Blue Cove and finds herself with people from an earlier time. She discovers that for generations there has always been a child in her family who understands "fog magic."

Playing Beatie Bow, by Ruth Park. Nelson, 1980.
Abigail thought Beatie Bow was a goofy kid's game played at dark to make it scarier until she discovered another girl was watching it, too. When she spoke to her, she found the streets of Sydney suddenly changed to cobblestone and an old-fashioned cab drawn by horses nearly ran over her.

Time at the Top, by Edward Ormondroyd. Parnassus, 1963.
At the top of her apartment house Susan finds a different world when one day she takes the elevator up, and it keeps on going! She meets people who live in a nineteenth-century Victorian mansion located in the same space as her apartment house.

Time Sweep, by Valerie Weldrik. Lothrop, 1978.

On a summer night in modern Sydney, Australia, a boy falls asleep in an old-fashioned bed and wakes up in London of a century earlier, having passed through a time warp that brings him friendship with a poor illiterate chimney sweep who shows him around London.

Tom's Midnight Garden, by Philippa Pearce. Dell, 1979.

Tom has to stay with relatives against his will, but the visit he dreads becomes a magical experience. One night when he hears an old clock strike thirteen, he gets up and wanders down to the back garden and begins his adventure.

A Traveller in Time, by Alison Uttley. Merrimack Book Service, 1981.

Penelope has a special gift of being able to go back and forth in time between the present and the time of Queen Elizabeth and Mary Queen of Scots while she is living in Thackers, her ancestor's manor house.

A Wrinkle in Time, by Madeleine L'Engle. Farrar, 1962.

Meg and her younger brother, Charles Wallace, learn that it is possible to get "caught in a downdraft and blown off course" in both space and time when they search for their father, a scientist who has disappeared while working on a special project for the government.

I Want Another
One That Goes On

THE "LITTLE HOUSE" BOOKS

Little House in the Big Woods, by Laura Ingalls Wilder. Harper,
1932.

Do you ever wonder how Laura got the nickname "half-pint?"
Have you heard about Pa's fight with the bear—that turned out to
be a tree stump? In this first book, you'll play "mad dog" with Mary,
Laura, and Pa; make maple sugar at Grandpa's; and start the long
journey to the *Little House on the Prairie.*

Little House on the Prairie, by Laura Ingalls Wilder. Harper, 1935.

Life on the high prairie is even more exciting than in the big woods
of Wisconsin. Laura and her family find that being surrounded by
a pack of fifty wolves and listening to Indian war drums in the night
are only a part of living in Indian Territory.

On the Banks of Plum Creek, by Laura Ingalls Wilder. Harper, 1937.

Their next home on Plum Creek in Minnesota is such a pretty
place to live, except when the creek floods in spring, or the grasshop-
pers come in summer and eat everything, or the blizzards come day
after day in the winter. Even when Pete the ox puts his hoof through
the roof of their sod house, Laura still loves it all.

NARNIA CHRONICLES

The Last Battle, by C. S. Lewis. Macmillan, 1956.

Under orders from a lazy, wicked ape, a donkey wearing a lion's skin masquerades as Aslan, bringing mischief to the land. Jill and Eustace see the end of Narnia, but Aslan leads them to a beautiful new land.

The Lion, the Witch and the Wardrobe, by C. S. Lewis. Macmillan, 1950.

Pushing aside the coats hanging in the wardrobe, Peter, Susan, Edmund, and Lucy first enter the enchanted kingdom of Narnia. Although Narnia has been spellbound by a wicked witch, the great lion Aslan breaks the spell, frees the country, and makes the four children its kings and queens.

The Magician's Nephew, by C. S. Lewis. Macmillan, 1955.

Cast into another world by his meddlesome uncle's magic rings, Digory and his friend Polly witness the creation of Narnia and all its creatures. The beautiful and evil Queen of Charn escapes her dying world and follows the children first to England and then to the world-being-born, Narnia.

Prince Caspian, by C. S. Lewis. Macmillan, 1951.

Back in England waiting to catch a train to school, the children suddenly find themselves magically sent to Narnia. They find that more than a hundred years have passed and that Narnia is now under the rule of Miraz instead of its rightful ruler, Prince Caspian, Miraz's nephew.

The Silver Chair, by C. S. Lewis. Macmillan, 1953.

Eustace and Jill are commanded by Aslan to find and rescue the lost heir to the throne of Narnia, Prince Rilian, who is captive in an underground kingdom and bound to a silver chair that has made him forget his true identity.

The Voyage of the Dawn Treader, by C. S. Lewis. Macmillan, 1952.

Edmund, Lucy, and their spoiled cousin Eustace return to Narnia and sail with King Caspian to find what became of the seven lords banished by Miraz. The islands to which they sail have treasures but also an enchantment that turns boys into dragons and water that turns anything it touches into gold.

PRYDAIN CYCLE

The Black Cauldron, by Lloyd Alexander. Holt, 1965.

Arawn uses the Black Cauldron to return to life the warriors slain in the battle between him and Gwydion, turning them into deathless beings who must do his bidding. As the best warriors of Prydain seek to destroy the cauldron, Taran learns that a high price must be paid to obtain it and a terrible price to destroy it.

The Book of Three, by Lloyd Alexander. Holt, 1964.

Frightened by the events she foresees, the oracle pig Hen Wen runs away into the forest. Taran, a young assistant pig-keeper, sets out to find her and finds himself drawn into the battle between Prince Gwydion and the forces of good and Arawn, lord of the Land of Death.

The Castle of Llyr, by Lloyd Alexander. Holt, 1966.

Sent to the Isle of Mona to be properly trained as a princess, Eilonwy is kidnapped by the enchantress Achren. When Taran, Prince Rhun of Mona, and others set out to rescue her, they are trapped first by a giant cat and then by its giant master.

The High King, by Lloyd Alexander. Holt, 1968.

Arawn captures the enchanted sword Dyrnwyn and assembles his forces for a final assault upon all of Prydain, including its High King. Against seemingly impossible odds, a small band, including Taran, rallies behind Prince Gwydion for a desperate stand against the evil Death Lord.

Taran Wanderer, by Lloyd Alexander. Holt, 1967.

Determined to find out the truth about his parentage, Taran, accompanied by the frightened but faithful Gurgi, sets out on a dangerous quest that takes him from one end of Prydain to the other. On the long journey, he finds danger, friends, and an identity.

WILL STANTON SERIES

The Dark Is Rising, by Susan Cooper. Atheneum, 1973.

On his eleventh birthday Will Stanton meets Merriman Lyon, one of the six Old Ones, those prophecied to save the world when the Dark, the forces of evil, rise. Will also learns that he himself is one of the Old Ones and wins an immortal talisman from a long-dead Viking king.

Greenwitch, by Susan Cooper. Atheneum, 1973.

When a chalice is stolen from the British Museum, Jane, Barney, and Simon go to Cornwall to help their great uncle search for it; and there they meet Will Stanton, a boy with strange powers. Greenwitch, a figure made of branches and thrown into the sea to bring luck, gives Jane a priceless gift.

The Grey King, by Susan Cooper. Atheneum, 1975.

In Wales recovering from an illness, Will Stanton finds all the elements foretold in a prophecy to waken the immortal Six Sleepers who are to ride against the Grey King and the forces of the Dark: a pale "raven boy" named Bran, his dog with silver eyes, and an enchanted gold harp.

Silver on the Tree, by Susan Cooper. Atheneum, 1977.

When Will blows his golden horn, the Drew children and Bran join forces with the Light as the forces of Dark rise to conquer the world. Light and Dark race to capture a crystal sword that will give one dominion over the other. A cosmic battle climaxes this epic.

I Want a
Song Book

SONGS

The Foolish Frog, by Pete Seeger and Charles Seeger. Macmillan, 1973.

Based on an old tune, this song is full of sound effects including clucking hens, squeaking barns, swishing grass, and bubbling brooks.

The Fox Went Out on a Chilly Night, an Old Song, illustrated by Peter Spier. Doubleday, 1961.

The fox takes a goose and a duck from the bin, and farmer John raises an alarm, but the fox runs to his warm den where he and his family feast.

Frog Went A-Courtin', retold by John Langstaff. Harcourt, 1955.

The flared claws and open mouth of "the old tomcat" destroy the serenity of the wedding feast of Froggie and Mistress Mouse.

Go Tell Aunt Rhody, illustrated by Aliki. Macmillan, 1974.

This is a popular song about a feather bed and the old gray goose who's dead.

Hush, Little Baby, illustrated by Margot Zemach. Dutton, 1976.

Whimsical Victorian people and creatures fill the pages of this visual interpretation of the beloved folk song.

Oh, A-Hunting We Will Go, by John Langstaff. Atheneum, 1974.

This popular, cumulative, participative song has been revived in this appealing edition in which you turn the page to guess the rhyme such as brantosaurus—chorus, and bear—underwear.

One Wide River to Cross, adapted by Barbara Emberley. Prentice-Hall, 1966.
The story of Noah and the Ark takes on new life as a spiritual.

10 Bears in My Bed: A Goodnight Countdown, by Stan Mack. Pantheon, 1974.
This well-known song features the usual ten bears in a very crowded bed who make their exits in peculiar ways such as roaring off on a motorbike, flying out in a plane, or roller-skating.

Yankee Doodle, by Edward Bangs. Parents, 1976.
The British soldiers sang "Yankee Doodle" to make fun of the American patriots, but after the defeat of the British, the Americans were singing the old song.

SONGS IN COLLECTIONS

American Folk Songs for Children, by Ruth C. Seeger. Doubleday, 1948.
This classic volume provides state origins, actions, and explanations along with piano accompaniment and chords.

Do Your Ears Hang Low, by Tom Glazer. Doubleday, 1980.
These fun songs have been known for generations, but it is often hard to find them written down. Besides the words and music there are ideas for actions.

Fireside Book of Folk Songs, by Margaret Boni and Norman Lloyd. Simon & Schuster, 1966.
These ballads, work songs, marching songs, carols, hymns, and spirituals come from around the world. A paragraph under the title tells you the song's country and origin.

The Fireside Book of Fun and Game Songs, collected and edited by Marie Winn. Simon & Schuster, 1974.
These surefire hits bring out the singing in everyone. The songs range from cumulative to chorus, from motion to two-part songs, from songs to be made up on the spot (nonsense, gruesome, and gross) to rounds and cheers.

The Fireside Song Book of Birds and Beasts, edited by Jane Yolen. Simon & Schuster, 1972.

The animals in these songs live everywhere—on farms, in houses, in the woods, air, and sea. This title offers easy-to-read musical notation for piano and guitar, a rich assortment of songs such as "The Darby Ram," an intriguing introduction to each selection, and appealing drawings in earth tones.

Glory, Glory, How Peculiar, compiled by Charles Keller. Prentice-Hall, 1976.

Fifteen school songs feature minor disasters, and the modern words are set to popular old tunes.

The Great Song Book, edited by Timothy John. Doubleday, 1978.

Tomi Ungerer's full-page paintings, with touches of his wry wit, are an added bonus in this book of sixty or more traditional songs with piano notations and guitar chords.

Hi! Ho! The Rattlin' Bog, edited by John Langstaff. Harcourt, 1969.

John Langstaff offers a full range of folk songs for group singing: ballads; processionals; dance tunes; part songs; and songs of the seas, the supernatural, and soldiers.

Sally Go Round the Sun, compiled by Edith Fowke. Doubleday, 1969.

Three hundred children's songs, rhymes, and games are musically notated.

I Want a Book
like Judy Blume's

Anastasia Krupnik, by Lois Lowry. Houghton, 1979.

Ten-year-old Anastasia gives her forthright, humorous commentary on current events in her life: a name that will not fit on a T-shirt, a wart on her finger, falling in love with Washburn Cummings, and awaiting the birth of her baby brother.

The Cybil War, by Betsy C. Byars. Viking, 1981.

From the moment he saw her, fifth-grader Simon knew that he was head over heels in love with Cybil Ackerman, but due to his best friend Tony Angotti's lies, Cybil has no love for him.

Dinah and the Green Fat Kingdom, by Isabelle Holland. Harper, 1978.

Moving to a new town, being thirty-two pounds overweight, and becoming jealous of a live-in cousin are all part of Dinah's twelfth year. In order to cope, she fantasizes and writes about a Green Fat Kingdom where fat is okay.

Felicia the Critic, by Ellen Conford. Little, 1973.

On target in her grasp of others' failings, Felicia brings about change for the good while stepping on some toes. She learns in some funny episodes that criticism can be helpful sometimes, and this encourages her to write to the president.

Harriet the Spy, by Louise Fitzhugh. Harper, 1964.

To help her to be a writer, Harriet keeps a secret notebook filled with caustic jottings about her parents, classmates, and neighbors. Her friends at school ostracize her when they find it, but even without her beloved nursemaid, Ole Golly, Harriet survives and learns to cope.

In Summertime It's Tuffy, by Judie Angell. Bradbury, 1977.

It is "Elizabeth" at home, but at summer camp it's "Tuffy." Tuffy's fourth year at summer camp is at Camp Ma-Sha-Na, where the girls even call her Tuf, but Alex asks her what her real name is.

It All Began with Jane Eyre; or, The Secret Life of Franny Dillman, by Sheila Greenwald. Little, 1980.

Franny Dillman's favorite Book is *Jane Eyre*. At her mother's insistence Franny tries some current teenage novels and starts keeping a diary of events around her. Her family is relieved to know that her dramatic revelations are her vivid imagination, better recorded in a book.

Operation: Dump the Chump, by Barbara Park. Knopf, 1982.

Eleven-year-old Oscar has had enough of his pesky younger brother Robert. Ever since he was born, Robert has been doing things to humiliate him, but a plan to get rid of Robert for the summer that Oscar devises somehow backfires.

Tomboy, by Norma Klein. Scholastic, 1978.

Ten-year-old Toe is beginning to feel the pains of growing up; moreover, her friends will not let her join their newly established Tomboy Club because they feel that she is not enough of a tomboy.

Where Are the Animal Books?

CATS

All about Cats as Pets, by Marjorie Zaum. Messner, 1981.
   Here is a book that has clear instructions and appealing photographs on how to play with your cat, vacation with your cat, feed your cat.

The Birth of Sunset's Kittens, by Carla Stevens. Addison-Wesley, 1969.
   When Sunset the cat gives birth to a litter of kittens, you are there for each exciting moment.

Cats, by Nina Leen. Holt, 1980.
   The different types of cats are featured, along with general information on cats at play and in history. The photographs are outstanding.

Cats: All about Them, by Alvin Silverstein and Virginia Silverstein. Lothrop, 1978.
   Cats through the ages, different breeds of cats, cats as pets—this title offers much information and advice as well as copious illustrations.

The Cricket in Times Square, by George Selden. Farrar, 1960.
   The lives of humans who operate a newsstand in Times Square are considerably enriched by the antics of a cricket whose musical talent teams up with the wisdom of Harry the Cat and the sophisticated patter of Tucker the Mouse.

F*T*C Superstar, by Mary Anderson. Atheneum, 1976.

Freddie the Cat comes back from his summer vacation completely stagestruck and ready to do *anything* to become an actor. Emma Pigeon, who can read and has a lot of clippings on acting, maps out a plan for his preparation. Can he make it on Broadway?

The Incredible Journey, by Sheila Burnford. Little, 1961.

Three pets—two dogs and a Siamese cat—set out on a journey through the Canadian wilderness to return to their original family. This trio, unused to anything but domestic life, endures many hardships.

King of the Cats, by Paul Galdone. Houghton, 1980.

A frightened gravedigger rivets his wife and friendly tomcat with a description of "nine black cats, like our friend Tom here," carrying a coffin and crying "miaiow."

Lights, Camera, Cats, by Judith E. Weber. Lothrop, 1978.

A girl arranges an audition for her cats to become television stars like Morris.

No Kiss for Mother, by Tomi Ungerer. Harper, 1973.

Piper, a self-centered tomcat, feels irreverent towards his mother—none of that sweetie-pie stuff for him!

Nobody's Cat, by Miska Miles. Little, 1969.

An alley cat leads a lonely life, even though there may be some excitement in it such as being cornered by a dog and escaping or being scared when a playful leap at a string turns on an electric light.

Socks, by Beverly Cleary. Morrow, 1973.

Socks the cat is jealous of Charles William, the new baby, who according to Socks is a pest, a feeling familiar to some brothers and sisters.

Star Ka'at, by Andre Norton and Dorothy Madlee. Archway, 1977.

Grieving over the death of his parents, Jim Evans wants only to be left alone until he meets the cat Tiro. But Tiro is no ordinary feline; a visitor from another world, he changes Jim's life.

DOGS

Big Red, by Jim Kjelgaard. Holiday, 1956.

The Canadian wilderness demands the utmost intelligence and courage from Danny and his dog Red.

Both Ends of the Leash, by Kurt Unkelbach. Prentice-Hall, 1968.

Unkelbach describes the ten best breeds for kids; clearly explains the mechanics of a dog show; and gives understandable, widely used instructions for the selection, care, and education of a puppy.

The Comeback Dog, by Jane R. Thomas. Houghton, 1981.

Although Daniel is sure he will never want another dog, he cannot resist trying to save the limp bundle he finds in the culvert. Does the dog want another boy? That is the question.

A Dog Called Houdini, by C. Everard Palmer. Andre Deutsch, 1979.

Trying to catch an escape artist like the dog Houdini means a wild chase for the townspeople and the dog catcher.

A Dog Called Kitty, by Bill Wallace. Holiday, 1980.

Terrified of dogs, Ricky at first wants to get rid of the stray puppy that he later learns to love.

The Hundred and One Dalmatians, by Dodie Smith. Avon, 1976.

As Pongo and Missis try to rescue the puppies that Cruella de Vil plans to turn into fur coats, our world is revealed as seen by knowing dogs.

Lassie Come-Home, by Eric Knight. Holt, 1978.

Times are so hard that even Joe's beloved dog Lassie has to be sold, and no one asks Lassie what she thinks about it all.

The Magic Moscow, by Daniel M. Pinkwater. Scholastic, 1980.

The combination of Norman Bleistift, a boy whose life is conveniently free of parents; Platinum Blazing Yukon Flash, a Malamute more often known as Edward; and an ice cream parlor called the Magic Moscow is frankly an invitation to read.

Mishmash, by Molly Cone. Houghton, 1962.

Mishmash turns out to be more dog than Pete can handle, and his very undoglike escapades startle the neighbors.

Morris Brookside, a Dog, by Marjorie W. Sharmat. Holiday, 1973.
When the elderly Brooksides urge their new dog to go out and make some new friends, he brings back a very dirty and unacceptable acquaintance.

The Puppy Book, by Camilla Jessel. Methuen, 1980.
There are many good photographs of Saffy, a retriever, as she has a litter of puppies and raises them.

Ribsy, by Beverly Cleary. Morrow, 1964.
From the time Henry Huggins' dog Ribsy is lost in a shopping center to the happy reunion a month later, he is fed, petted, and coddled by a variety of people from whom he manages to escape.

Scruffy, by Jack Stoneley. Random, 1979.
A stray dog whose adventures are both dangerous and funny, Scruffy becomes the most famous dog in Great Britain.

Some Swell Pup, by Maurice Sendak and Matthew Margolis. Farrar, 1976.
Two children try yelling, spanking, and even the West Pointer Academy when their new puppy does not behave perfectly until a wise passerby helps them to mend their ways.

Superpuppy: How to Choose, Raise and Train the Best Possible Dog for You, by Jill Pinkwater and Daniel M. Pinkwater. Houghton, 1976.
Thinking of getting a puppy or training the one you have? This book tells you how to choose, train, care for, and understand a dog.

The Trouble with Tuck, by Theodore Taylor. Doubleday, 1981.
A guide dog for a *dog*? When Tuck, a Labrador Retriever, goes blind, his owner tries to train him to follow a companion dog.

Where the Red Fern Grows, the Story of Two Dogs and a Boy, by Wilson Rawls. Doubleday, 1961.
There are twenty-five sets of hounds in the coon hunt in the Ozark Mountains, but Little Ann and Old Dan compete heroically to win the cup and the prize money. Later when they fight a mountain lion, the first tragedy, Old Dan's death, occurs.

HORSES

The Black Stallion, by Walter Farley. Random, 1944.

A wild black horse and a boy survive a storm at sea. Rescued from an island, the boy helps tame the Arabain stallion.

The Blind Connemara, by C. W. Anderson. Macmillan, 1974.

Rhoda is offered the chance to help the beautiful white pony that is going blind when it is given to her. Her patience wins the little pony's confidence.

The Book of Horses, by Glenn Balch. Scholastic, 1967.

Different kinds of horses such as Morgans, Arabians, and Tennessee Walkers are introduced, and good information is included on learning to ride and the best way to care for a horse of your own.

Can I Get There by Candlelight? by Jean S. Doty. Macmilan, 1980.

While riding Candy, her gray pony, Gail meets Hilary, who offers to teach her to ride sidesaddle. They become friends; but when Gail tries to retrieve Candy's bridle, she cannot get through the rusty gate as before, and she realizes then that Hilary could only have existed in a previous time.

Cowardly Clyde, by Bill Peet. Houghton, 1979.

When put to the test, the timid war horse Clyde overcomes his fear and rushes back to save his master. The cartoon-like pictures are colorful and energetic.

The Girl Who Loved Wild Horses, by Paul Goble. Bradbury, 1978.

An Indian girl spends all the time she can with the horses in her village. During a storm the frightened horses stampede and carry her to a wild herd. She becomes enchanted by their leader, a wild stallion, and forsakes her people to remain with him.

King of the Wind, by Marguerite Henry. Rand McNally, 1948.

The mute Arabian stable boy cares for the Godolphin Arabian, ancestor of Man o' War, on his journey across the seas to France and England; and Agba is chosen to be in the saddle when the horse is honored by the Queen.

A Morgan for Melinda, by Doris Gates. Viking, 1980.

Ten-year-old Melinda has a fear of riding horses, so when her father buys her a horse, it is the last thing she wants. However, with the help of a friend, Melinda learns to overcome her fear.

A Pictorial Life Story of Misty, by Marguerite Henry. Rand McNally, 1976.

A fantastic collection of photographs is supplemented by Wesley Dennis's sketches and Marguerite Henry's biography of Misty.

Summer Pony, by Jean S. Doty. Macmillan, 1973.

The summer pony is a pathetic-looking animal that has been rented for Ginny for her vacation. Under her loving if inexperienced hand, Mokey turns into a respectable pony.

Thunderhoof, by Syd Hoff. Harper, 1971.

Thunderhoof is a wild horse who does not want to be tamed by the cowboys. When he finally does escape, he realizes he would rather stay with them.

A Very Young Rider, by Jill Krementz. Knopf, 1977.

The narrative and the black-and-white photographs successfully capture the world of Vivi, a competitive and enthusiastic ten-year-old rider.

The Wild Ponies of Assateague Island, by Donna K. Grosvenor. National Geographic Society, 1975.

Annually, the wild ponies of Assateague Island are taken to Chincoteague Island to be sold as children's pets.

Wonders of the World of Horses, by Sigmund A. Lavine and Brigid Casey. Dodd, 1972.

This general study of a variety of horses is devoted primarily to their history and physiology and to the distinguishing characteristics of different breeds.

Year of the Black Pony, by Walt Morey. Dutton, 1976.

Oregon frontier life seems bleak for Christopher until his stepfather buys him the spirited black pony of his dreams. Christopher's mother is against the transaction, but she rallies to the horse's aid when it catches pneumonia.

ODD ANIMALS

Alligator, by Evelyn Shaw. Harper, 1972.

How the American alligator lays and protects its eggs, avoids hunters, and makes it through the winter are shown.

Animal Fact/Animal Fable, by Seymour Simon. Crown, 1979.

Do rats desert a sinking ship? Can you tell the temperature by a cricket's chirp? These and other beliefs about animals are proven or refuted in this colorful picture book.

Bats, the Night Fliers, by Anabel Dean. Lerner, 1974.

Bats are the second largest group of mammals in the animal world, and many people are afraid of them. Their habits, characteristics, sonar ability, and in the case of three types of bats, bloodsucking techniques are explained.

Gorilla, Gorilla, by Carol Fenner. Random, 1973.

The life of a gorilla is poetically told from its birth and youth in East Africa to its capture and placement in a zoo.

Hawk, I'm Your Brother, by Byrd Baylor. Scribner, 1976.

To glide effortlessly like a hawk is Rudy Soto's greatest wish. He even captures a baby hawk from its nest to foster a kinship. However, Rudy senses the growing bird's yearning to fly and turns him loose. Vicariously, Rudy shares the experience of flying, and the two become "brothers."

The March of the Lemmings, by James R. Newton. Harper, 1976.

In the Arctic North lemmings, hamster-like rodents, eat and multiply until a hidden call starts their march to the sea.

Owls in the Family, by Farley Mowat. Little, 1961.

Wol and Weeps are two little owls who become beloved but mischievous pets in the Mowat family in Saskatoon, Saskatchewan.

The Remarkable Chameleon, by Lilo Hess. Scribner, 1968.

This little ground lion cannot really turn plaid, but it is an expert at camouflage and hiding from its enemies. It can also swivel its eyes around independently. How it changes color, reproduces and lives, and how to keep one as a pet are covered.

A Snail's Pace, by Lilo Hess. Scribner, 1974.

Concentrating on the common land snail, Hess gives all the vital information about its life and life cycle and then goes on to describe the more exotic kinds.

PIGS

The Amazing Bone, by William Steig. Farrar, 1976.

On her way home from school, Pearl the pig discovers a talking bone that saves her from robbers and an awful fox. The bone gets an honored place in Pearl's home, and the whole family enjoys talking to the bone and sometimes hearing music from it.

The Book of the Pig, by Jack D. Scott. Putnam, 1981.

The pig is presented as intelligent and amiable and, would you believe, even liking to be clean.

Charlotte's Web, by E. B. White. Harper, 1952.

This is almost as much Wilbur's story as it is Charlotte's. He is "Some Pig" in this barnyard account of love and devotion even unto death.

The Peppermint Pig, by Nina Bawden. Harper, 1975.

"What's a peppermint pig?" Poll asked, thinking of sweets. "Not worth much," her mother told her, "runt of the litter. But even runts grow." It does; and it steals hot cross buns and gooseberries, becomes a famous pig, and makes one whole year for Poll a special memory.

Pigs Wild and Tame, by Alice L. Hopf. Holiday, 1979.

Black-and-white photographs show bushpigs, warthogs, peccaries, and some others along with the barnyard pig.

Pinch, by Larry Callen. Little, 1975.

Pinch, a country boy, makes a series of trades and ends up with a pig. He trains it to be a hunting pig, and it wins an important local contest in spite of trickery and gets a special apple pie as a reward.

A Treeful of Pigs, by Arnold Lobel. Greenwillow, 1979.

The wife would like some help taking care of the pigs, but her lazy husband says he will help only when pigs grow in trees like apples. His wife outsmarts him, and he ends up doing his share.

The Witch's Pig: A Cornish Folktale, by Mary Calhoun. Morrow, 1977.

Cousin Tom is mistaken when he thinks he has outwitted Betty in acquiring the pig she wanted. He does not believe she is a witch until everything goes wrong trying to raise the pig. Betty gets the pig cheap from Tom, and Tom resolves never to tangle with Betty again.

SHARKS

Album of Sharks, by Tom McGowen. Rand McNally, 1977.

Full descriptions, including color paintings, of eleven species and brief glimpses of other strange sharks show that the word "shark" covers a variety of creatures. True stories such as a five-hour battle with a seventeen-foot great white and legends such as how a Hawaiian boy tricked a shark are included.

A First Look at Sharks, by Millicent Selsam and others. Walker, 1979.

What makes sharks different from other fish and some of the ways to know different sharks from each other are given.

Focus on Sharks, by Sarah R. Riedman and Elton T. Gustafson. Harper, 1969.

Detailed information on the individual members of the shark families includes scientific and popular names, appearance, and habits. Black-and-white photographs show details such as how the nictitating eyelid works or how a shark gives birth. Charts of shark attacks around the world are included.

Hungry Sharks, by John F. Waters. Harper, 1974.

A good bit of scientific information emphasizes the shark's anatomy, especially the use of its senses to find food. The book also stresses the importance of scientific observation.

Hunting the Killer Shark, by Otto Penzler. Troll, 1976.

The dangerous work of marine researchers who "hunt" sharks with cameras and recording equipment, to learn more about them and to test shark repellents, is described.

Nightmare World of the Shark, by Joseph J. Cook and William L. Wisner. Dodd, 1968.

Written from the fisherman's viewpoint, this book has photos of dead sharks and a chapter on fishing gear and techniques. It also includes legends from around the world and recent stories by hunters.

Sand Tiger Shark, by Carol Carrick. Houghton, 1977.

This is the story of one of a pair of twin sand tiger sharks as it is born, grows, mates, and hunts until the fatal day when it is accidentally slashed during a feeding frenzy and becomes the victim of another shark, a great white.

Savage Survivor: 300 Million Years of the Shark, by Dale Copps.
  Follett, 1976.
After beginning with a vivid description of a shark attack on a
swimmer, Copps describes the shark's physical characteristics and
abilitites and its value and danger to people, citing the research of
many marine scientists.

Shark Lady: True Adventures of Eugenie Clark, by Ann McGovern.
  Scholastic, 1978.
When nine-year-old Eugenie, who spent Saturdays at the aquari-
um, grows up, her dream of studying fish comes true. Her adventures
include studying caves with "sleeping" sharks, discovering a shark
repellent, and even carrying a live shark to Japan as a present for the
crown prince.

The Shark: Splendid Savage of the Sea, by Jacques Y. Cousteau and
  Philippe Cousteau. Doubleday, 1970.
The stories and color photos are ones of the sharks encountered
by the divers from the ship *Calypso:* blue sharks attack a baby whale
injured by the ship's propeller; two divers tagging small sharks have
a narrow escape when a huge one suddenly appears; and another
diver gets the ride of his life by hanging onto a whale shark.

Sharks, by Rhoda Blumberg. Watts, 1976.
Some vivid descriptions of shark encounters are included along
with the descriptions of a number of kinds of sharks such as the
basking, blue, and hammerhead. Sharks have companions and enemies, too; and these are described as well.

Sharks, by Herbert S. Zim. Morrow, 1966.
Sharks evolved four hundred million years ago and are related to
skates and rays. Brief descriptions of twenty sharks are included with
sketches of the head, skeleton, skin, and intestines. The ways in
which their vitamin-rich liver oils, their rough skin, and teeth are
used are also discussed.

SMALL ANIMALS

Abel's Island, by William Steig. Farrar, 1976.
Abel, a young mouse used to the easy life, is separated from his
wife in a storm, swept away, and marooned on an island where he
spends a lonely and difficult year as a castaway.

Basil of Baker Street, by Eve Titus. McGraw-Hill, 1958.

Basil is an admirer and student of Sherlock Holmes. Although not 100 percent successful, he is in many ways a mouse copy of the real Holmes.

Ben and Me, a New and Astonishing Life of Benjamin Franklin as Written by His Good Mouse Amos, lately discovered, edited, and illustrated by Robert Lawson. Little, 1939.

A self-important mouse narrates his claims for all the credit for Benjamin Franklin's fame. The premise is amusing, and the book is all the funnier because you can see that the mouse's ideas are more disastrous than successful.

The Champion of Merrimack County, by Roger W. Drury. Little, 1976.

This mouse is a daredevil cyclist who finds his ideal racetrack in an antique bathtub. A crash, mouse traps, ferocious cats, and all kinds of plotting are overcome to get O. Crispin safely back on his bicycle.

Chipmunks on the Doorstep, by Edwin Tunis, Harper, 1971.

Tunis presents more than seventy drawings of chipmunks in life-like color.

The Cricket in Times Square, by George Selden. Farrar, 1960.

Chester, a country cricket, accidentally lands in the middle of New York City where he is befriended by Tucker Mouse, Harry Cat, and the Bellini family, all as different as can be.

The Great Rescue Operation, by Jean Van Leeuwen. Dial, 1982.

After the Dolly-Deluxe doll carriage at Macy's is sold with Fats the mouse asleep in it, Marvin and Raymond, two other mice, discover how difficult it is to find a two-inch, two-pound mouse in New York City.

House Mouse, by Oxford Scientific Films. Putnam, 1978.

House Mouse shows with excellent pictures where the animal lives, what it eats, how it mates, and how it develops from a hairless newborn to a mature adult.

The Island of the Skog, by Steven Kellogg. Dial, 1973.

After a hard getaway and some rough sailing, Jenny and the Rowdies find an island to live on—only the mice seem to be sharing their home with a large monster!

Miss Bianca, by Margery Sharp. Little, 1962.

A girl needs rescuing; and a diamond palace, a wicked duchess, twelve mechanical ladies-in-waiting, and two heroic mice are involved.

The Mouse and the Motorcycle, by Beverly Cleary. Morrow, 1965.

Ralph's craving for the motorcycle and his friendship for the boy who won it put him in danger of vacuum cleaners, dogs, and discovery by the wrong people.

Mrs. Frisby and the Rats of NIMH, by Robert. C. O'Brien. Atheneum, 1971.

When her family is threatened, Mrs. Frisby, a mouse, seeks help from the mysterious and highly intelligent rats of NIMH. The plans they mastermind offer her a solution but also require her help.

Stuart Little, by E. B. White. Harper, 1945.

Stuart is an unusually bold and independent little person who looks like a mouse, born into a human family. His love for a bird named Margalo leads him on an adventure-filled quest.

A Summer in the South, by James Marshall. Houghton, 1977.

Eleanor Owl, the famous detective, cannot seem to get away from mystery, even when she's on vacation.

The Wild Rabbit, by Oxford Scientific Films. Putnam, 1980.

An amazing amount of information on wild rabbits' habits—burrowing, mating, raising their young, and eating—is shown in beautiful full-page colored photographs with simple captions.

Winter Story, by Jill Barklem. Philomel, 1980.

Elated by the first heavy snowfall in many years, the mice of Brambly Hedge build a fabulous Ice Hall and hold a Snow Ball.

WILD ANIMALS

Elsa, by Joy Adamson. Pantheon, 1961.

Elsa is taken from the book, *Born Free*, a true story of a lioness that Joy Adamson and her husband, a senior game warden, rear from cubhood and teach to stalk and kill for herself so that she can be set free in the African jungle.

Gentle Ben, by Walt Morey. Dutton, 1965.

When Mark befriends a huge brown bear in Alaska, the future looks bleak for this odd friendship because people are afraid of Ben and do not understand the bond between Mark and the wild bear.

Goblin, a Wild Chimpanzee, by Geza Teleki and Karen Steffy. Dutton, 1977.

Eating leaves, seeds, and berries, playing alone and with his friend Pom, exploring the world around him as he and his mother Melissa move about the forest, meeting other chimpanzees and baboons, hunting termites and gathering figs—even being chased and very nearly killed by a buffalo—are all part of Goblin's day, which ends with building a nest in a tree and going to sleep.

The Grizzly Bear with the Golden Ears, by Jean C. George. Harper, 1981.

A mother grizzly bear and the cub, whom she loves more than anything else, live in the Northwest wilderness where they are at home, fishing for food in the river. After she loses and then finds her cub, the mother moves to another river.

The Midnight Fox, by Betsy C. Byars. Viking, 1975.

The summer his folks bicycle through Europe, Tom grudgingly stays with his aunt and uncle on their farm. Life is dull until he spies a black fox and her cub and studies their life styles.

Nature's Pretenders, by Alice L. Hopf. Putnam, 1979.

Animals of all kinds use pretense to attract others or to keep off their enemies. The clear photographs show various kinds of camouflage and other aids.

The Owl and the Prairie Dog, by Berniece Freschet. Scribner, 1969.

If you have ever wondered about life underground, this brief account of a burrowing owl and her neighbors will interest you.

Pandas, by Donna K. Grosvenor. National Geographic Society, 1973.

Visit bamboo forests high in the mountains of China to see giant pandas in their native habitat and then go to the National Zoo in Washington, D.C. and enjoy watching our own pandas, Ling-Ling and Hsing-Hsing.

Rascal: A Memoir of a Better Era, by Sterling North. Dutton, 1963.

A Wisconsin farm boy and his playful pet raccoon named Rascal enjoy a year together before Rascal is returned to his natural home.

Red Fox, by Charles G. Roberts. Houghton, 1972.

A boy watches and admires a red fox in the Canadian backwoods; the fox's life story is accurate nature lore.

Wild Animals of North America. National Geographic Society, 1979.

Absolutely irresistible for all ages, this excellent book is crammed with a great deal of information and color pictures.

The Wolf, by Michael Fox. Coward, 1973.

Dr. Fox, an authority on animal behavior, follows two wolves from the birth of a litter through the first year of their cubs' lives. Fox emphasizes wolves' intelligence and their affection and respect for one another as well as the part they play in the balance of nature.

Author-Title Index

Frances Laverne Carroll is a professor of library science at the University of Oklahoma where she teaches courses on children's literature and international librarianship. She served formerly as supervisor of school libraries in Coffeyville, Kansas. She is the author of *Recent Advances in School Librarianship* and series editor of Reading for Young People, published by ALA.

Mary Meacham, a free-lance writer and editor, is currently a doctoral candidate at Texas Woman's University. She has taught courses on children's literature at the University of Oklahoma and worked as a children's and young adult librarian. She is the author of *Information Sources in Children's Literature* and the compiler of *The Northwest* in the Reading for Young People series.